Praise for

Homemade for Sale

Revive local economies and create jobs. Add value instead of selling commodities. Rebuild regional food systems. Diversify production on the landscape. Capitalize the infrastructure for a sane and healthy diet. And yet, there is no switch to flip: we have to start-small, learn the lessons, and grow this sector ourselves. *Homemade for Sale* is the perfect start. The many thousands of food entrepreneurs today making magic in their home kitchens and brushing elbows with farmers in packing sheds, are tomorrow's locally owned processing companies, making tomato sauce for school lunch, and jelly for the local deli's sandwiches. Like seedlings and piglets, big things start small, from the ground up, and that means you and me, and the kitchen sink. Yes, we can!

—Severine vT Fleming, director, Greenhorns; and co-founder, Farm Hack and National Young Farmers Coalition

The *ECOpreneuring* team has done it again! Over the years, they've given us several indispensable authoritative guidebooks, but make note, their how-to writing style is uniquely playful and inviting. Lisa and John don't just invite you into their world, they suck you in. By the time you finish reading *Homemade for Sale*, you'll be wearing your farmers-market-John/jam-n-jelly-Jane hat in total confidence.

—MaryJane Butters, author, *Milk Cow Kitchen*, MaryJanesFarm.org

Imagine for a minute what an extra $5,000 or $10,000 or more a year would mean to you and your family. If you could earn that money doing something you already love, right from your own kitchen, how would that change your life? This isn't some late night infomercial — this is micro-entrepreneurship made possible by recent Cottage Food legislation. Lisa and John's latest book, *Homemade for Sale*, is a practical, tactical guide to help you turn your beloved hobby into a profitable, small-scale business. This step can feel like an intimidating leap, but *Homemade for Sale* is like the experienced friend that takes you in hand and shows you the path from here to there. If you have a passion for creating and sharing, you can have a business. Lisa and John show you how, with direct, expert advice on Cottage Food regulation, the day-to-day realities of business cash-flow management, marketing, branding, packaging and more. *Homemade for Sale* is an indispensable guide to joining the Cottage Food industry, avoiding common pitfalls and building a thriving business from your own home. Profiles of successful micro-entrepreneurs show the many ways people are successfully creating their own cottage businesses, and if you ever outgrow the "cottage", *Homemade for Sale* covers how to scale up and join the world of commercial food production. Cottage Food legislation is the promise that almost anyone can become a businessperson and grow their own diverse income stream with almost no start-up cost or risk. *Homemade for Sale* shows you how to turn that promise into a successful, satisfying reality.

—Erica Strauss, *Northwest Edible Life*, (www.nwedible.com)

Homemade for Sale is an inspiring guide for anyone interested in starting a home-based food business. Lisa and John have been through the fire themselves and scoured the cottage food industry to find the best resources to help you get off the ground and succeed. From understanding your state's laws to incorporating your business to choosing the right products customers to market to, they take you step by step through everything you should be doing and thinking about. Their profiles on other cottage food entrepreneurs bring everything a little closer to home and may be just the motivation we all need to take part in the movement ourselves.

—Lev Berlin, Founder ReciPal

Having answered thousands of cottage food-related questions, I can confirm that this book fills a void that the internet does not. I've seen many cottage food operations making tasty products with bland profits, and *Homemade for Sale* correctly focuses on the missing ingredient — marketing. It will give your new business an edge in a crowded marketplace. Well-researched, loaded with examples, and perfectly tailored to the home cook, this book will point you in the right direction. For any first-time food entrepreneur, *Homemade for Sale* isn't recommended reading... it's required.

—David Crabill, co-founder, Forrager Inc.

We are in a golden age for local, artisanal culinary products. But the food industry can be particularly challenging for startup businesses. *Homemade for Sale* is a valuable resource to help culinary entrepreneurs understand what lies ahead so they can more easily navigate their journey of turning their passion into a livelihood.

—Gregory Heller, author, *U.S. Kitchen Incubators: An Industry Snapshot*

Many of my readers and students ask me for advice on starting a cottage food business. I'm thrilled to recommend *Homemade for Sale* as it is a comprehensive volume full of helpful legal knowledge to practical business and marketing advice. This is an essential for anyone ready to make the leap to launch their food business.

—Kate Payne, author, *The Hip Girl's Guide to Homemaking* and *The Hip Girl's Guide to the Kitchen*

Lisa Kivirist and John Ivanko answer all the questions that you need to know about starting your own food business! This book is an amazing compilation of the current food laws and trends and will give any person interested in pursuing a career in food the upper hand. The research is strong and the writing witty with a perfect combination to make *Homemade for Sale* a must for any foodie, homesteader or dreamer. I wish this book came out 12 years ago when I was starting my own business as it would have given me a great upper edge!

—Jordan Champagne, co-founder and co-owner, Happy Girl Kitchen Co.

What an insightful look at the cottage food industry. Food entrepreneurs receive useful direction — taking them from their idea's inception to finished product in this first authoritative guide of it's kind. Thank you for promoting Good Food with *Homemade for Sale*.

—Jim Slama, President, FamilyFarmed

Homemade FOR SALE

HOW TO Set Up AND MARKET A Food Business FROM YOUR HOME KITCHEN

Lisa Kivirist & John D. Ivanko

new society
PUBLISHERS

Cover design by Diane McIntosh.
Cover images: Top right, Mixing Bowl © iStock impactimage;
Middle three: © John Ivanko; Bottom right, Scales: © iStock fasphotographic;
Illustration — Cooking Utensils © iStock ma_rish.

Printed in Canada. Second printing June 2015.

New Society Publishers acknowledges the financial support of the Government of Canada
through the Canada Book Fund (CBF) for our publishing activities.

Paperback ISBN: 978-0-86571-786-2
eISBN: 978-1-55092-582-1

Inquiries regarding requests to reprint all or part of *Homemade for Sale*
should be addressed to New Society Publishers at the address below.

To order directly from the publishers, please call toll-free (North America)
1-800-567-6772, or order online at www.newsociety.com

Any other inquiries can be directed by mail to:
New Society Publishers, P.O. Box 189, Gabriola Island, BC V0R 1X0, Canada
(250) 247-9737

New Society Publishers' mission is to publish books that contribute in fundamental ways
to building an ecologically sustainable and just society, and to do so with the least possible
impact on the environment, in a manner that models this vision. We are committed to doing
this not just through education, but through action. The interior pages of our bound books
are printed on Forest Stewardship Council®-registered acid-free paper that is **100% post-
consumer recycled** (100% old growth forest-free), processed chlorine-free, and printed with
vegetable-based, low-VOC inks, with covers produced using FSC®-registered stock. New
Society also works to reduce its carbon footprint, and purchases carbon offsets based on an
annual audit to ensure a carbon neutral footprint. For further information, or to browse our
full list of books and purchase securely, visit our website at: www.newsociety.com

Library and Archives Canada Cataloguing in Publication

Kivirist, Lisa, author
     Homemade for sale : how to set up and market a food
business from your home kitchen / Lisa Kivirist & John D. Ivanko.

Includes index.
Issued in print and electronic formats.
ISBN 978-0-86571-786-2 (pbk.).--ISBN 978-1-55092-582-1 (ebook)

     1. Food industry and trade--Management. 2. Food industry and trade--Marketing.
3. New business enterprises--Management. 4. Home-based businesses--Management.
5. Home-based businesses--Marketing. I. Ivanko, John D. (John Duane), 1966-, author II.
Title.

HD9000.5.K49 2015   664.0068'1   C2014-906422-5
                                                C2014-906423-3

To food entrepreneurs across the country, who have been pickling, baking, preserving and blending some of the most delicious food products we've ever savored. Your home kitchens rock!

Disclaimer

THIS BOOK IS DESIGNED TO AND MAKES EVERY EFFORT to provide accurate information. It's sold with the understanding that neither the publisher nor the authors are engaged in rendering legal, accounting, or other professional services. Each person's legal or financial situation is unique, as is the application of the law to the facts with the fair and reasonable interpretation of them. Any action pursued related to the contents of this book should be undertaken with the counsel and advice of a trained legal, tax, investment, and accounting professional. Because of the risk involved with an investment of any kind, neither the publisher nor the authors assume liability for any losses that may be sustained by the use of the advice described in this book, and any such liability is hereby expressly disclaimed. If legal or other professional assistance is required, the services of a professional should be sought, especially since some of the information could, and likely will, change because it relates to governmental tax law and its interpretation thereof.

Contents

Section 2: Selling Your Story: Marketing

Section 3: Organizing, Planning and Managing the Business

Acknowledgments

FOOD IS SYNONYMOUS WITH COMMUNITY. We enjoy sharing every jar of pickles or loaf of zucchini bread with friends, family and our bed and breakfast guests. We love the land, the delicious treats that can be created from our harvest of it and the grins that accompany every bite.

This book champions community too. Without the amazing creativity, passion and talents of home cooks everywhere, our sense of taste would go dormant. The food you create in your home kitchens are what this book both celebrates and inspires. Special thanks to those cottage food entrepreneurs who graciously shared their stories for this book: Felicia Hill (FH Cakes), Erin Schneider and Rob McClure (Hilltop Community Farm), Isa Lunsford (Sweet Pick Me Ups Bakery LLC, LCC), Jennifer Evans (Cookies Plz), Suzy Zimmermann (Queen of Cake and Events), Rhonda L. Jones (Chez Moi Bakery), Barbara Preston (Hana Lulu's Candy), Regina Dlugokencky (Seedsower Farm), Dorothy Stainbrook (HeathGlen's Farm & Kitchen) and Liz James (The Happy Tomato). Nell Newman couldn't have set the tone for the book better.

Thanks, also, to David Crabill of Forrager.com, who helped put cottage foods on the map and continues to guide the movement by providing a directory, a forum for discussion and a quick reference guide to what's happening in every state. Appreciation goes out to Rachel Armstrong, founder and executive director of Farm Commons, for her legal insight and savvy support for small-scale farmers looking to diversify into value-added products. We offer a shout out to the Wisconsin Farmers Union for collaboratively supporting our efforts to expand the cottage food legislation in our state to include baked goods through the Cookie Bill. Thanks also to the Midwest Organic and Sustainable Education Service (MOSES) and Renewing the Countryside for championing our work and the voices of rural food and farm businesses.

Without the talents of our editor, Scott Steedman, and the visionary guidance of New Society Publishers — Ingrid Witvoet, Sue Custance and

Mary Jane Jessen, and all the marketing folks — our book would be nothing more than a half-baked idea. And once again, Diane McIntosh designed the perfect cover.

Finally, to our son, Liam, we cannot thank you more for your patience as Mom and Dad pecked away at the keyboard — and your never-ending sense of humor, which kept us laughing. While our parents, Aelita and Walt Kivirist and Susan Ivanko, may never have created a product in their own kitchens for market, their skills behind the counter provided the foundation for our culinary career today. They say you learn most by example, repeated over and over again.

Foreword

by Nell Newman

WHEN I WAS 5, MY PARENTS MOVED FROM AN APARTMENT IN NY to an old farmhouse in Westport CT. I still remember our first visit to this house, my mother, my father and me, and how enamored we were of "the country." The farmhouse had an old apple orchard on one side, and a smoothly flowing stream behind it. Beyond that, the woods hummed with life. Although we frequently spent time in LA, the farmhouse in Westport became home and a source of many fond memories.

A large part of these memories revolved around food. No matter where we were, my parents tried to make dinner a family event where we were always asked to be part of the preparations. In the summer, we always bought our produce from Ripey's Farmstand, where it was my father who taught me the rich smell of a perfect cantaloupe and the fullness of a good ear of corn. We had apples from our trees for pies and applesauce and eggs from the two New Hampshire Reds.

Both of my parents loved to cook, and each had their specialties. The family rule was that you always had to try what was served at meals. That was how I came to love my mother's artichokes with hollandaise sauce (made with our chickens' eggs).

My father was a smart man, not a foodie per se, but he did like to cook his set of specialties. He was more of a technician in the kitchen than a cook, even with something simple like a hamburger. The fat content had to be 19-21%, and run through the grinder no more than 3 times, he told the butcher. Burgers were to be carefully formed and never squished while on the grill.

Setting up the barbecue was half comedy, half science. He was always trying out new techniques often employing a blow dryer or oscillating fan, "you know, to get the coals just right." He insisted that we cut the tomatoes with a serrated knife, "nice thick slices" he would say.

To tell you the truth, I can't remember a time that Pop didn't make his own salad dressing. When we lived in New York, one of our favorite places

to eat was a wonderful little restaurant called Madame Romaine De Lyons. Madame's specialized in omelets with approximately 200 different kinds, handwritten in her menu. Accompaniments included a croissant or brioche, a small salad of romaine lettuce with an incredibly piquant Dijon dressing and French pastries for dessert.

Although I was very young when Madame passed away, I remember that each time we ate there my father always complimented her on her salad dressing. One day he asked her if she might be willing to share it with him. She claimed it was a secret and that she couldn't possibly part with it. Shortly thereafter, Pop sent her a pair of autographed pictures of my mother and him — and the recipe was passed on.

Although it's been many years since Madame's closed, I still remember the acidic bite of her traditional Dijon dressing. Pop's was similar but different. As I was young, and salad dressing wasn't in my repertoire and I couldn't say exactly how he made it his own, but I do recall the use of celery salt, which used to be called Beaumont.

Over the years, he refined his recipe, experimenting with different kinds of olive oil until he was satisfied. That salad dressing was what I ate on a daily basis, and it was what we served to guests who came to visit. Guests and friends enjoyed it so much that they clamored for a little bottle of it to take home.

One year Pop decided to give his salad dressing away for Christmas in hand-labeled wine bottles. They were a huge hit, and once again, his friends all clamored for more.

After a few years, the demand became so great that he decided to look into manufacturing his salad dressing. The first few bottling plants he called told him a minimum run was 30,000 cases, and that realistically, celebrity products always failed. Pop took that as a challenge, so he approached a local grocery store called Stew Leonards. Stew told Pop that he would take the whole run. It sold out in one year, leaving Pop with $890,000 worth of profit.

In 1982 that was a lot of money. Pop, at the peak of his career, decided to give it all away. He did so quietly, mainly to small non-profits. "If people knew how good it felt to give their money away, they wouldn't wait until they were dead to do it," he told me one day.

The main reason that Pop's salad dressing did so well was because it tasted so much better than the usual run-of-the-mill bottled dressings. It also didn't have preservatives, artificial flavors or colors, because as Pop said, "I don't use those things at home. Why do I need them now?" That was very unusual for the mid 80s, and it was the true meaning of "all natural".

Pop, of course, was the most surprised by his success, as evidenced by the Newman's Own motto, "If we have a plan, we're screwed." It was kind of true in a way. He and his business partner A.E. Hotchner pretty much started the whole thing on a whim and flew it by the seat of their pants for quite some time.

About 21 years ago, I made my father a delicious organic Thanksgiving dinner, which gave him the confidence to help my business partner and me start another division of Newman's Own. Newman's Own Organics raised the bar on the flavor of organic snacks. At the same time, we introduced millions of people to food made primarily with ingredients grown without chemicals.

That said, you don't have to fly by the seat of your pants like Pop did. *Homemade for Sale* can help you jumpstart your food business, guide your dream and help you make it a reality. Instead of salad dressings, perhaps your products are cookies, jars of jam or pints of pickles.

My childhood exposure to delicious, wholesome ingredients probably got me into my parent's kitchen and cooking, which led to my starting a business that used that skill nicely. Whatever your particular gift is in the kitchen, explore what you can do with it... You never know what could happen!

Good Luck!

Nell Newman,
Co-Founder of Newman's Own Organics

Nell Newman.

Introduction: Cottage Food Freedom

"Like clockwork every Christmas, my family loves my special gingerbread cookies and tells me I could make money selling them, but I don't know where to start."

"I have so many extra tomatoes from my garden each summer. It'd be great to sell some salsa."

"I love baking, but I really have no interest in starting a full-time bakery, especially being a stay-at-home mom with young kids. But doing something part-time from my home kitchen. That's something for me."

"There's nothing more satisfying than making and sharing my fruit jams and jellies with others. I keep giving everything away, but my friends tell me they'd be happy to buy from me. But I don't have big bucks to start a full-blown commercial operation."

"My husband keeps telling me that I need a project. We're retired, but I don't like playing golf or fishing. I feel at home in the kitchen and have a knack for creating yummy treats for my husband and his friends. Starting a food business sounds like it might be fun and rewarding."

CAN YOU RELATE TO ANY OF THESE ENTHUSIASTIC HOME COOKS? If so, you're not alone.

You could be part of a growing movement of people starting small food businesses from their homes. No capital needed, just good recipes, enthusiasm and commitment, plus enough know-how to turn ingredients into sought-after treats for your local community. Everything you require is probably already in your home kitchen. Best of all, you can start tomorrow!

1

Cottage Food Freedom

Thanks to new laws currently on the books in more than forty-two US states, small-scale food businesses can now be operated from home kitchens. These state laws, often referred to as "cottage food legislation" or "cottage food laws," have nothing to do with cottage cheese and everything to do with allowing you to sell certain food products to your neighbors and community. By certain foods, the laws mean various "non-hazardous" food items, often defined as those that are high-acid, like pickles, or low-moisture, like breads. Because of this definition, some of the state cottage food laws have been nicknamed Pickle Bills, Cookie Bills or Bakery Bills on their journey to becoming laws where you live.

While no one claims to have invented the term "cottage food," its meaning is clear. A cottage is small and handcrafted, typically one story tall, no more, and designed with simplicity and modesty in mind. That definition forms the essence of these modern cottage food laws, enabling us to step away from the industrialized and factory-based food systems that engulf our world today toward a more authentic and tastier time filled with unique, homemade items from small food artisans. At their heart, today's cottage food laws allow us to do much more than just launch individual businesses. They provide the catalyst for transporting our society back to an era when everyone bought locally from trusted neighbors.

With most of the cottage food laws passed since 2008, states make it possible for anyone to earn income, follow a culinary passion or dream, and have some fun. How? By selling specific food items made in your home kitchen. From pies to pickles, wedding cakes to granola, preserves to decorated cookies, fledgling food entrepreneurs no longer need to sink more than fifty thousand dollars into a commercial kitchen or fork over fifty dollars an hour to rent a licensed facility to turn Aunt Emma's biscotti recipe into a money-making dream business. We now have the freedom to earn.

The new cottage food laws make home kitchen enterprises the next hot small business trend, accessible to anyone with a passion for food. So turn your ribbon-winning state fair strawberry rhubarb pie or "famous within your family" fudge into an enjoyable business that can earn you some money to pay off those credit card balances or save for a rainy day. With millions of Americans living paycheck to paycheck, never has it been easier to moonlight out of your kitchen to make ends meet. Perhaps you'll even

"Starting a food-oriented small business can be more than just a dream. If you want to package and sell your soup, jam, candy or grandma's salsa, you'll find many customers willing to try your new taste sensation, plenty of places such as farmers' markets to sell your product, and believe it or not, you can have low start-up costs."

— RHONDA ABRAMS, *USA TODAY* (NOVEMBER 29, 2013)

Canada's "Cottage Food" Conundrum

At the time of writing, there are no general national or provincial "cottage food laws" (or pending bills) in Canada.

"The Canadian Food Inspection Agency provides regulatory oversight with respect to many aspects of food and related products in Canada, including, for example, labeling and packaging requirements for these products," explains Carly Dunster, a food lawyer with Carly Dunster Law (carlydunsterlaw.com), based in Ontario, Canada. "The federal government has also passed new legislation entitled the *Safe Food for Canadians Act*, coming into force in 2015, that will consolidate a number of federal food laws and which demonstrates an increased emphasis on food safety at the federal level.

"It is conceivable that someone could create a commercial kitchen in their home, but the requirements are onerous, both in terms of just the physical infrastructure you would need and in terms of the zoning," continues Dunster. "For example, you can't operate a commercial kitchen out of your home unless your house is zoned commercially, which isn't typical. The federal organization that regulates food is the Canadian Food Inspection Agency (inspection.gc.ca), but the operation of a commercial kitchen would, in many ways, be governed by provincial and municipal regulations and public health agencies."

Another source of further information related to food preparation is the Canadian Restaurant and Foodservices Association at their website, crfa.com.

However, in some provinces, there are specific cases — if you operate a farm, for example, and want to sell specific non-hazardous food items made in your home kitchen at a farmers' market, community market, charity fair or similar "temporary food market" — you may be allowed to do so. Consult with your local health authority.

In British Columbia, according to the "Guideline for the Sale of Foods at Temporary Markets", April 2014, from the BC Centre for Disease Control (bccdc.ca), an agency of the Provincial Health Services Authority, lower-risk foods prepared in home kitchens are allowed to be sold to the public at temporary markets, like farmers markets. Additional requirements include, but are not limited to, the following:

- Lower-risk food means food in a form or state that is not capable of supporting the growth of disease-causing organisms or the production of toxins. One or more of the following factors usually apply to these foods:
  - Water activity (Aw) of 0.85 or less, or
  - A pH (hydrogen ion concentration) value of 4.6 or less.
- Vendors of home-prepared foods at temporary food markets must only sell foods that are considered to be lower risk. Vendors are allowed to sell home-prepared lower-risk foods at temporary food markets without contacting or receiving approval by the local Health Authority.

☛

- Vendors of lower-risk foods are not required to submit an application before commencement of sales. It is the vendor's and the market manager's responsibility to ensure that all lower-risk foods meet the definition of a lower-risk food.
- Public health is protected by ensuring that food prepared at home which is offered for sale at temporary food markets is limited to lower-risk foods.
- A sign is displayed that is clearly visible to the consumer at the point of sale stating that "THIS FOOD HAS BEEN PREPARED IN A KITCHEN THAT IS NOT INSPECTED BY A REGULATORY AUTHORITY," or equivalent wording.
- Pets should be excluded from kitchens during the time food is being prepared.
- Home-prepared/packaged food may be subject to Canadian Food Inspection Agency and Health Canada requirements for allergens, labeling, weights and measures. Vendors are advised to check with their local CFIA office to ensure their packages/labels comply with applicable federal requirements.
- The following list contains examples of **lower-risk foods** that may be **acceptable** for home preparation and sale at a temporary food market:

  - Apple sauce
  - Brownies
  - Bread and buns (no dairy or cheese fillings)

- Butter tarts
- Pies (fruit-filled only, no cream-filled or cream-based)
- Cakes (icing sugar only, no dairy or synthetic whipped cream)
- Dry cereal products
- Chocolate (provided it is used for re-melted or re-molded products only and (1) not purchased from bulk bins; (2) sourced from a chocolate manufacturer that can provide a certificate of assurance that chocolate is free from Salmonella).
- Cinnamon buns (sugar icing only)
- Cookies
- Dried fruits
- Fresh fruits and vegetables
- Fudge
- Hard candy
- Honey
- Jam and jelly (pH 4.6 or less or Aw of 0.85 or less)
- Muffins (no dairy fillings)
- Popcorn
- Noodles (dry flour and water only, no egg based)
- Pickled vegetables (vinegar base, pH 4.6 or less)
- Relish (vinegar base, pH 4.6 or less)
- Wine and herb vinegar
- Syrup
- Toffee
- Salsa (if pH and Aw within acceptable ranges and the food contains no animal protein. If whole or cut tomatoes are ☛

used as an ingredient, then the pH of the final product must be less than 4.2.)

"We sell wood-fire-baked sourdough bread, plus syrups, sauces, salsa, both pressure and water bath-canned, all produced from our vegetables and fruits," says Denise Cross of Mountain Valley Farm (mountain-valleyproduce.com) located in West Kelowna, British Columbia. She operates the "beyond organic" farm with her husband, Tom, and son, Brandon, making all their products in their farmhouse kitchen. "We sell all of the products at both our Farmgate Market and the local farmers' market."

"We've determined to take it one step at a time, practice what we preach and share our belief in respecting ourselves and our environment with the next generation, our neighbours, our customers and our community," adds Tom Cross. "Our goal is to invite, support and share with all who believe there is importance in real food."

A similar exemption for farmers to sell value-added, non-hazardous foods at a farmers' market exists for Ontario as well. According to the Niagara Region Public Health (regional.niagara.on.ca), "A special exemption is provided at farmers' markets to allow vendors to sell non-hazardous home prepared products. This exemption is not applicable to any other commercial facilities or events. The purpose of this exemption was to allow farmers at a farmers' market to sell a variety of products made from their own produce or fruit (i.e., jams, jellies, pies)."

sell enough goodies to cover that family vacation you always wanted but could never afford.

As the first authoritative guide to launching a successful food enterprise operated from your home kitchen, *Homemade for Sale* provides a clear roadmap to go from idea and recipe to final product. It offers specific strategies and resources for people running home-based food businesses, unlike other books that focus on commercial baking or food

"If you've been spending the holiday season whipping up goodies to share with family and friends, you might have caught yourself wondering whether you could turn your prize-winning peppermint bark or mouthwatering marmalade into a tasty sideline business or retirement income. Maybe so. In fact, this is a great time to savor the increasing opportunities for food entrepreneurs. Consumers are embracing specialty and artisanal foods like never before."

— Nancy Collamer, *Forbes*

product businesses. As defined by the law, your business, at least when you start, will be a part-time, small-scale operation operated by you.

Work Your Passion for Food

What do Paula Dean, Martha Stewart and Mrs. Fields have in common? They all started their business from their home. Like you, they share a passion for food and chose careers in the kitchen that they love.

Flash forward to today. Most of the forty-two states that have cottage food laws in place passed these after the Great Recession of 2007; they were viewed as a relatively low-cost option to spur entrepreneurial start-ups. With minimal, if any, inspections or registration processes, cottage food laws can be administered by state agencies for much less than the costly inspections required of full commercial operations.

Because these laws are so new, little information is available regarding the number of cottage food start-ups and their sales. However, during the first year that California's law was in place, more than 1,200 new businesses registered. Arizona is home to more than 2,400 cottage food operators. Data on other states is far more elusive. Ranging in size, sales and product offerings, these businesses would not have legitimately existed be it not for the cottage food laws passed.

Many food entrepreneurs are drawn to the cottage food industry because they love cooking and love the autonomy that comes with minding their own business and being their own boss. Perhaps you share this perspective. Are you tired of punching the clock and would rather punch some dough?

As it turns out, budding home kitchen entrepreneurs come in many persuasions and myriad motivations. Which one best defines you?

- Dream-catcher, eager to fulfill a lifelong dream of running a small food enterprise.
- Home baker, possibly with seasonal specialty items you want to share with your community.
- Stay-at-home mom wanting to earn extra income while keeping an eye on the kids.
- Someone with food sensitivities or allergies, who, after years of struggle, has found delicious recipes that work for you and might work for others, too.

"Allowing for cottage food operations is an easy way that states can support the development of small businesses and increase the availability of local products within their borders. The fact that forty-two states allowed some sort of in-home processing of non-potentially hazardous foods demonstrates that these types of operations are important and valuable to the citizens of those states.

"As more consumers become interested in supporting local food economies and more producers begin starting their own food businesses, states need to make sure that those local businesses can survive and thrive. Although many states have cottage food or home-based food processing laws on their books, there are still a number of ways in which states can update and improve their cottage food regimes to match the growing demand and opportunity for cottage food operations."

— HARVARD FOOD LAW AND POLICY CLINIC, A DIVISION OF THE CENTER FOR HEALTH LAW AND POLICY INNOVATION

- Dedicated locavore foodie, wanting to make a difference in the local food movement beyond your shopping habits.
- Retiree looking to stay relevant and active, plus make a little extra "fun money."
- Specialty cake and wedding cake maker looking for a chance to share your artistic talent and creative flair.
- Farmer looking to diversify your business by offering bread and other items at farmers' markets to boost your revenue.
- Economic survivalist who has found that Plan B, despite a college degree, is the new Plan A.
- Career changer from breadwinner to bread baker, looking to test your food-based dream before you quit your day job.
- Someone between jobs and searching for a quick way to earn some cash to pay the bills.

As we talked with cottage food business owners across the continent, we discovered that launching a small food enterprise could be for anyone and everyone. While our non-scientific sample tended to skew female, there are plenty of men too, and food entrepreneurs are both young and old and come from various ethnic or socioeconomic backgrounds. They live in urban, suburban and rural places. All share a passion for the culinary arts.

Starting a food-based enterprise from your kitchen is an incredible opportunity, whether it resulted from politicians feeling the heat to do something as a result of the financial fallout from the Great Recession, was spawned by the "buy local" movement or came about because of pressure from the 99 percent who want to sell items directly to their neighbors and make a little money without wading through government regulations.

To help spur and support home-based food enterprises, many state governments decided to cut the excessive red tape and allow people to get to work and earn some money by becoming small business owners. In other words, they allowed Americans to be what Americans have always been: enterprising, community-focused and hard-working. Forget the unemployment lines, food pantries or minimum-wage McJobs. Make way for the muffin makers!

Perhaps encouraging cottage food businesses makes plain common sense. That's the way things were done in America for more than a century:

"Lots of people are eyeing their kitchens right now as a way to earn a little extra cash in a bad economy."

— Emily Maltby, CNNMoney.com
(July 2009)

neighbors selling to neighbors; fellow parishioners selling to fellow parishioners; local businesses selling to local residents. It's how business was done before the age of cheap oil, industrialization and globalization.

First-timer or Seasoned Pro?

We wrote *Homemade for Sale* as a comprehensive and accessible reference guide for home cooks unacquainted with operating a small business, as

Buy Local and Sell Local

Our kitchen is the place we feed those who matter most to us: our family. We do so with love, care and safety in mind. Would we really do anything differently when serving the public?

We can thank our current industrialized food system for the shift from homemade goodness to factory efficiency and the resulting disconnect from what we put into our mouths. Flash back to our pioneering "Little House on the Prairie" era when life centered on the hearth and home kitchens. You purchased those few staples you didn't raise on your homestead from the Oleson's Mercantile in town, a spot where you knew the shopkeepers, even their irritating daughter, Nellie.

But as our country increasingly modernized, embracing the lure of cheap, factory-made products, food safety lost out. Horrid working conditions and unsafe food products rose to the public's priority list in the early twentieth century with the publication of Upton Sinclair's book *The Jungle,* a classic tale of the horrific conditions in the Chicago meat-packing industry. *The Jungle* influenced the laws that followed to regulate and clamp down on the food industry. While desperately needed at the time, these same laws

have since been amended, expanded and interpreted so broadly that public schools now ban homemade items for classroom birthday treats.

Today's cottage food movement cooperatively supports the burgeoning "buy local" movement across the country. The economic evidence of revitalized local community food systems is coming in. According to the Institute for Local Self Reliance, in a comparison study of local and national chain retailers, the local stores return a total of 52 percent of their revenue to the local economy, compared to just 14 percent for the chain guys. Similarly, local independent restaurants recirculate an average of 79 percent of their revenue locally, compared to only 30 percent for chain eateries.

The same process can happen with cottage food businesses. Buy your ingredients from a locally owned, independent grocery store or food cooperative and sell your products to folks in your neighborhood, then return to the store and buy more flour, butter or canning jars. The money circulates within your community. You're not just a small, home-based chutney-producing business, you're playing a role in changing our economic system, one cookie and neighbor connection at a time.

well as a more detailed book for business-savvy, but first-time, food entrepreneurs. Some of you reading this book may just need a little nudge to hang out your shingle. With you in mind, we've created the chapter Make It Legal: Establish Your Business in 7 Easy Steps. For more seasoned entrepreneurs, we've offered several chapters on marketing, drawing from our experiences over the years in the public relations and advertising fields; we've worked at the full-service Leo Burnett Advertising Agency and know a bit about Tony the Tiger and Ronald McDonald. We write press releases for various clients as well as feature articles for national magazines, working both sides of the aisle.

We also include plenty of guidance and resources that should help business owners eager to diversify or expand with new products they can sell to the public by leveraging cottage food laws. Personally, we're tapping the cottage food law in Wisconsin to sell pickles, preserves and other high-acid canned items to guests staying at our Inn Serendipity Bed & Breakfast. If all goes as planned and our state's legislation expands to include baked goods, combined, this could mean a bump of five thousand dollars a year in revenues. In other words, in a business as small as ours, it could be the difference between operating at a profit or a loss. As we explore at length in our other books, *Rural Renaissance, ECOpreneuring* and *Farmstead Chef*, we define success in ways far beyond financial wealth or prestigious corner offices or titles.

As a Cottage Food Operator, or CFO, you're in charge and responsible

Cottage Food Pros and Cons

Pros	Cons
Little to no capital needed; you probably have everything you need in your kitchen already.	State regulations limit what products you can make, some more than others.
Fast start-up. Most states have a simple, low-cost registration process.	States may also have limitations on where you can sell; some do not allow special orders and restrict sales to farmers' markets or public events.
May already have a recipe and be experienced in what you want to make.	
Sell directly to the customer and keep more profit.	With any food product, you're liable for what you make and need to insure yourself for the risk you take.
There's nothing like the flexibility and freedom of being your own boss — you get to call your own shots.	Baking, canning and other food preparation is hard work on your feet, especially if you have to make multiple fresh items at once.
You're helping build a stronger local economy and community connections.	
Defining success on your own terms.	Bookkeeping is a must since you're required to keep track of sales, expenses and inventory. A real chore, if you don't like crunching numbers.
Opportunity to grow and expand *after* you prove a successful market.	May stir up some negative vibes when viewed as competition by local businesses like an established commercial bakery.

for the outcome of your endeavor. This can be empowering and unnerving, satisfying and trying. It can also be enriching, in every sense of the word. When you operate your home-based food business, you can make some money, do what you want and, maybe, even make a difference in your community.

It's Thyme. Why Now?

From Buy Local to Small Business Saturdays, from slow food to fancy food, from farm-to-fork to handmade artisan breads, more people than ever are demanding real food made by real people — not by machines in factories, the same way they make cars and computers.

The growth of farmers' markets, specialty food products and farm-to-table restaurants that source their foods directly from farmers, fisherman or food artisans reflects this hunger for foods with ingredients we can pronounce, made by people who live at places we could visit, maybe even in our home town. Below are a few more trends worth considering:

- Organics are growing 9 percent annually. More than 81 percent of US families say they are trying to buy some things organic, according to the Organic Trade Association.
- The specialty food business grew more than 22 percent between 2010 and 2012, according to the Specialty Food Association. The two most likely characteristics of new products include gluten-free food (38 percent) and convenient/easy-to-prepare items (37 percent).
- Farmers' markets continue to grow, with a 3.6 percent increase from 2012 to 2013, totaling 8,144 markets in the US, according to the USDA's Agricultural Marketing Service.
- The cake and bakery market continues to rise at an average annual rate of nearly 5 percent, according to the industry research firm IBISWorld. The reason we're eating so many cupcakes? While disposable income dropped during the recession, perhaps people turn to these luxury food items as an inexpensive way to indulge.

Let's be real. As more research findings surface on the improved health, nutrition and taste of products made from real ingredients, the greater the demand for these products made with no preservatives, artificial flavors or colors or mystery ingredients courtesy of the science lab. While laws labeling ingredients or products as containing genetically modified organisms (GMOs) have remained elusive, retailers are demanding transparency when federal and state governments do not. Whole Foods Market, for example, declared that by 2018, all products they sell must state whether they contain GMOs or not.

Added to this are the growing issues more Americans have with respect to what they eat. Allergies or sensitivities to peanuts, soybeans, gluten and dairy products have exploded. More on this in Chapter 2.

Cottage food enterprises address these growing trends, solving problems and meeting customer needs like few large corporations ever could. As a result, these micro enterprises often have a competitive advantage — beyond minimal regulations of the cottage food laws themselves. Their small size, direct connection and responsiveness to customer needs and attentive detail to each and every product are beyond large food companies.

While food products from most corporations are designed for shelf life, transportability, uniformity and profitability, cottage foods, by their very nature, are small batch, fresh and specialized. Fewer and fewer Americans are being fooled by mega-food producers' product labels that read fresh from the oven, all-natural, homemade goodness, artisanal. And more of us have discovered that Betty Crocker is a make-believe person created by the marketing department of General Mills.

Do you laugh when you hear Duncan Hines claim their cookie mixes are "Chewy, gooey, homemade good"? Or General Foods Corporation proclaiming "like grandma's, only more so"? While these mega-corporations feel the need to create an image of homespun goodness, your venture, by default, *is* authentic, transparent and real. In our murky world where distrust runs rampant, the idea that someone can buy direct from someone they trust has a deep emotional appeal. It's much easier and simpler to trust the food you put in your body when you're on a first-name basis with the person who made it.

It's probably illegal, or practically impossible, to ever visit most animal-processing facilities, commercial farming operations or processing factories, where the vast majority of the food Americans eat is currently made. By selling to neighbors, co-workers or community members, cottage food enterprises promise to usher in a new era of accountability and transparency not seen since the days of *Little House on the Prairie*.

"The food industry is more crowded than ever with new players entering the field every day. In order to be successful you must differentiate yourself by having a clear value proposition and a strong story that resonates with your consumers. As a small business your greatest asset is your ability to connect on a human level with your customers. That is something the larger brands simply can't do in an authentic manner and something that many food entrepreneurs overlook. Focus on building strong connections with your customers and engage them in conversation be it at the farmers' market, at the side of your food truck, or online via social media. Invite them to be part of your food business journey and they will reward you with their loyalty."

— 2014 PLATE OF THE UNION REPORT,
SMALL FOOD BUSINESS (SMALLFOODBIZ.COM)

"Avoid food products containing ingredients that are (A) unfamiliar (B) unpronounceable (C) more than five in number or that include (D) high-fructose corn syrup."

— MICHAEL POLLAN, *IN DEFENSE OF FOOD: AN EATER'S MANIFESTO*

Left:
*Slow Rise Organic Bakery,
Gabriola Island, Canada.*
Mary Jane Jessen

Right: *Rolls on a conveyor
system.* iStock: © Wicki58

Key Elements of Cottage Food Laws

By their very nature, most cottage food businesses are:

- small-scale, grossing under $2,000 in revenue, at least starting out;
- independent and family-run, usually by only one person;
- home-based and use the equipment they already own in the kitchen.

So with your only expenses being a license or two and perhaps a few safety checks, depending on your state, you may be able to get going with an investment of less than a couple of hundred dollars. Producers operating under cottage food legislation save costs and enjoy the ease and convenience of working from home rather than having to rent or build a commercial kitchen, as required in commercial food-processing regulations.

As well as some licensing steps, your state cottage food laws will specify what kind of sales, sales venues and types of foods are permitted. Plus, your state will tell you exactly how much you can earn with your business.

Nationally, this sales cap ranges from five thousand dollars on the very low end to the majority of states with unlimited caps where you could earn as much as you want from the comfort of your home. There are more than a dozen states with extremely open-ended laws that not only have no sales caps but also allow sales both direct to the customer and indirect (or wholesale) to places like retailers or restaurants.

Organization of this Book

Homemade for Sale is broken into four sections. In the first section, What's Cooking?, we address in greater detail what cottage food laws allow, help you evaluate your goals and offer tools to navigate your state's regulations and get you going with refining your ideas and recipes. Cottage food regulations vary tremendously from state to state in terms of what you can produce, where and how you can sell it and how much gross income you can bring in. There's a patchwork of rules and regulations, and not all states have laws in place. This section will sort this all out, helping you focus on the ideas with the biggest potential. If you live in Canada, where no cottage food laws exist other than specific provincial exemptions related to farmers selling non-hazardous food products made in their home kitchens at farmers' markets, skip to the fourth section, Scaling Up, to see if you want to go directly to some form of commercial kitchen setup.

The second section, Selling Your Story: Marketing, covers everything from developing your product, its packaging and label to sharing the story you create around it on a website or with your co-workers in the form of a flyer. While the tendency is to focus on the product, say your family's favorite salsa recipe, when you're selling to the public, what you sell must ultimately satisfy the needs of your customers, aka "the market." Good marketing will increase your likelihood of success, which is why this section of the book is the most detailed.

The next section, Organizing, Planning and Managing the Business, gets into the nitty-gritty of setting up your business, putting together a simple plan, organizing your kitchen and putting together any production or operational systems you'll need to keep your business in good shape, including legally and personally.

Finally, we'll close with a section that addresses if, or when, the time comes to expand your business beyond your kitchen headquarters. In

Scaling Up, we'll examine what to do if your amazing products appear to be the Powerball of the cottage food lottery, with sales growing to the point that they hit the gross sales cap for cottage food enterprises or are simply too high for your kitchen space to handle. You'll have to decide whether you want to keep it cottage-food-small or expand your enterprise. We'll explore scaling up your operations along a continuum, from a modest investment to a tens-of-thousands-of-dollars commitment.

If you think you have the kind of products that can be sold nationally — and have the financing, research and personal interest to take it to the next level — we'll briefly cover some potential next steps and point you toward resources and books that focus on these large-scale, full-time food enterprises. If all goes as planned and you get a little bit of luck along the way, your product may end up on the shelves of Costco or Hannaford, the largest certified-organic supermarket in the Northeast.

For the majority of *Homemade for Sale* readers, however, keeping things small and home-based will be the recipe for success: a perfect blend of an independent, entrepreneurial enterprise that shares a love for cooking with their local community.

Since there's such a patchwork of state laws and diversity of home-based food entrepreneurs, *Homemade for Sale* features ten inspiring "story profiles" of cottage food start-ups and the people behind them. The people profiled address real-life challenges while sharing practical advice and opportunities about starting the business. Every major direct sales channel and cottage food category is represented, including decorative cookies, wedding cakes, pickles, breads, preserves, candy, cupcakes, shrubs, tomato marinara sauce and salsas. In many cases, the profiles reveal specific financial, legal and operational issues often absent in other start-up books.

The cottage food movement represents more than an income source or a fun new project. You're helping to grow the local food movement in your community by providing "direct-to-the-food artisan" connections. *Homemade for Sale* celebrates this and, as you read further, provides a pragmatic blueprint for success as you launch your dream food venture — right from your home kitchen!

Finally, "homemade" and "fresh from the oven" mean exactly what's written.

What's Cooking

SECTION 1

1

Navigating Your State's Cottage Food Law

THIS CHAPTER WILL HELP YOU NAVIGATE your state's cottage food law. If you don't have such a law that allows you to sell what you'd like to your neighbors, we'll touch on that, too. At the time of writing, there are eight states and every Canadian province (other than some specific farmer exceptions for sales at farmers' markets) with no cottage food law at all.

Tips for Understanding a Cottage Food Law

The following tips serve as a guide to understanding your state's cottage food law.

(1) *Review Your State's Cottage Food Law*

Cottage food laws are typically administered by a state's department of agriculture or whatever department regulates "food production." This is usually not the same department that regulates and inspects facilities that prepare and serve food, like restaurants or catering operations. In some states that require a kitchen inspection, this would often be administered through the state's department of health. There's a big difference between "production" and "preparation" — so much so that each is handled by a completely different department with a completely different set of rules, regulations and procedures.

Another key difference between the two involves "service." Once you start selling and serving a food item you made, the regulations and requirements immediately become more complex, often involving refrigeration, serving temperatures, food handling, licensing issues and sanitation. Stick to just selling the whole chocolate cake. When you start slicing and selling individual cake pieces along with a fork, you add another layer of regulations and cost. An easy workaround: offer cupcakes if you want to sell individual servings.

In Wisconsin, for example, the Department of Agriculture, Trade and Consumer Protection administers the cottage food law. However, the Wisconsin Department of Health and Human Services administers, inspects and licenses establishments that prepare and serve food to the public, like

Direct-to-customer or Indirect (Wholesale)

While each state's cottage food laws vary on multiple levels, every law specifies to whom the product can be sold. This "to whom" then falls into two categories that probably sound familiar: direct and wholesale. Direct means directly to your customer. You, as a baker of brownies, sell some to me, the customer. I pay you directly and then, happily, am the one to eat them, give them as a gift or do whatever else I choose to do with them, as long as I do not resell them.

Indirect sales, sometimes referred to as wholesale, cover a wide range of other sales opportunities. If you live in a state that allows wholesale, you could potentially sell me those brownies and I could then resell them at a venue like my retail store or coffee shop. While you receive a lower price for wholesale transactions, the benefit is higher volume and, hopefully, more regular orders. Brownie sales at the farmers' market fluctuate and can tank if a summer thunderstorm rolls in. If you know my coffeehouse will buy four dozen brownies a week, you often gross more revenue despite the lower price due to economies of scale and a reliable stream of orders flowing in.

More than a dozen states have passed laws that permit sales on a wholesale level. As an added bonus, these states often permit other food categories like refrigerated baked goods, and generally don't have a sales cap either. Bottom line to your bottom line if you're fortunate enough to live in one of these states: you get to create close to a commercial kitchen arrangement without the cost and setup hassle such a facility often entails. In general, however, such states have more upfront requirements, including an on-site kitchen inspection and paperwork. Once you work through these, you can operate under a much wider range of product possibilities.

Sometimes laws legalizing wholesale products produced in home kitchens come bearing names other than cottage food. Instead, they might have the word "home" in the law title. Make sure you know the right way to refer to this classification if you want to pursue it further or call the administering agency for clarification. In Iowa, for example, the law is called a Home Food Establishment; in Maine, one of the first states to institute such a law more than thirty years ago, it's referred to as a Homestead License. California's law, passed in 2012, refers to cottage food but breaks it down into two classes of licensing: Class A-licensed operations can only sell direct to customers, but Class B operators have options to sell wholesale.

The consistent variable among states permitting wholesale remains the ability to use a home kitchen in a more commercial capacity. If wholesale interests you, ask about the possibilities, knowing those laws may be defined in ways other than as cottage food.

restaurants, caterers and even our bed and breakfast. Can you see where things can get confusing?

(2) *Stick to Your State as Your Primary Source of Information*

In journalism, articles can be sourced from primary or secondary sources. Primary sources are the people, companies or organizations directly involved with the topic; secondary sources are people or organizations that may report about a subject. Primary sources of information are always preferred to secondary sources. That's one reason why Wikipedia can never be used as a source.

Forrager (forrager.com) is an online cottage food community. It contains information about the cottage food laws, includes a directory for cottage food operations, and allows people to connect and share ideas about the industry.
Map courtesy of Forrager Inc (forrager.com)

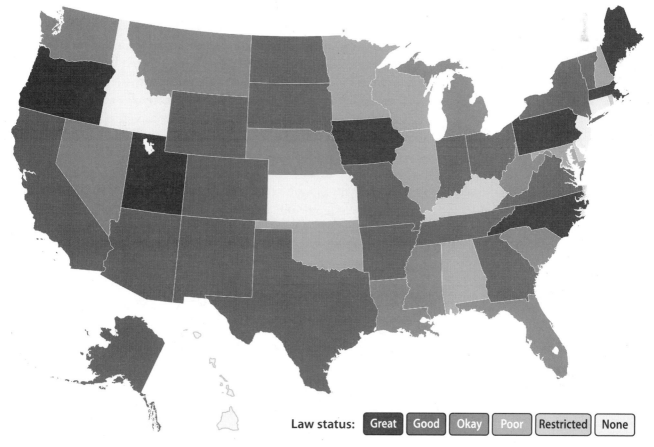

Cottage Food Laws in the United States

Law status: Great Good Okay Poor Restricted None

As cottage food laws grow in number across the country, websites are popping up to address the hunger for information about them, filling gaps where states often fall short: in providing readily accessible, easy-to-understand content. Such websites can also be a great way to connect with other food entrepreneurs in your state since they might offer an online forum for discussions. The best example is forrager.com.

While cottage food websites are a quick reference point with lots of useful information, avoid basing your information solely off them; they could become outdated, contain factual errors or suddenly disappear one day. In other words, these sites are secondary sources of information, perhaps more valuable to marketing than keeping tabs on what's happening in your state.

Your state's current cottage food law should be the only thing to direct the scope of your business. Treat it as your primary source. Remember, you are responsible for the actions of your business. The decisions you make must be based on the law as it stands. Avoid decisions based on what you hear or what someone else may be doing, particularly if it's in another state.

Throughout this book, we use illustrative examples based on laws that may change in the coming years. Change is constant, especially when it comes to legislatures creating, repealing and amending laws. The great news is that cottage food laws are mostly bipartisan. Both Republicans and Democrats tend to agree on the importance of job creation, employment and encouraging the growth of small business. Where they have a hard time working together and agreeing is on how.

Some states' cottage food laws are simple and short while others go on and on. These two extremes express two different approaches to writing laws. A shorter, more general law will enable the administering body (i.e., your state's department of agriculture) to address and answer questions and issues as they come up. A more detailed law aims to answer everything up front but leaves little wiggle room for questions or alternative interpretations. Keep this in mind when reviewing your state's law.

(3) *Tap State Resources to Understand the Law*

You only have to deal with and understand your state's cottage food law. Some states have accessible, user-friendly and easy-to-understand information on their cottage food law. Not all do. Depending on your state, you'll find yourself either muddling through some technical data and legal verbiage or proceeding easily with clearly defined guidelines and requirements. When in doubt, contact the department or agency directly to sort out issues and get advice on your specific product idea and your next steps.

States that truly embrace cottage food law opportunities couldn't make it easier, with a checklist approach to guide new food entrepreneurs. In the case of laws about pickles, preserves and other canned products, university extension will often serve as a more objective educational arm and offer various online resources and in-person workshops and consultations. Don't, however, count on university extension agents giving you the definitive yes or no to your product; they're not lawyers or administrators of the law, nor may they have a talent for marketing.

In states with more clunky and hard-to-understand information, you'll need to educate yourself on the more technical terms used in cottage food legislation as it applies to your product.

If you feel like you're getting a runaround to your questions from the department handling the cottage food law — or no reply at all — go to the top! Contact your state elected representative and/or senator to see if they or their staffers can help. There's nothing more powerful to jump-start a less-than-responsive governmental office than a letter from your representative.

A word of caution, however, when dealing with legislators. You may need to bring your representative up to speed on the cottage food law. In your initial contact, it would be wise to reference the specific law and what you hope to accomplish in their district with your business. Making money and paying some taxes are two good selling points. Most politicians like to hear from their constituents, too. Don't forget to include your full address (not a PO box) when contacting your representatives.

Quart-sized jars of Inn Serendipity pickles with cucumbers raised on the authors' farm. John D. Ivanko

(4) *Follow Your State's Registration and Review Process*

What do you need to do specifically to get your business started? This can vary considerably from state to state. Some states require annual registrations, licensing fees and food safety training. Most require some form of business registration. We cover the seven easy steps to starting up your business in Chapter 11.

Self-Taught Cake Maker Doesn't Make Peanuts

Name: Felicia Hill

Business: FH Cakes
(Vancouver, Washington)

Website: fhcakes.com

Products: designer cakes

Sales Venues: direct and custom orders

Annual Sales: nearing $15,000 gross
sales cap

Felicia Hill pulling a cake out of her oven.
COURTESY OF FH CAKES

"All I wanted to do was bake a cake for my son," shares Felicia Hill with a laugh. "I never dreamed it would grow into this." This determined suburban mom took her young son's need for a peanut-free birthday cake and channeled it into a thriving business, FH Cakes. Along the way, she pioneered the cottage food industry in the state of Washington.

"Back in 2008, I couldn't find a bakery in town that was peanut-free and could create any kind of cake for my son, Daniel, who has a severe peanut allergy," explains Hill. Having no other option than to do it on her own, Hill took on the challenge and signed up for the basic Wilton cake-decorating class at the Michaels craft store chain to learn the basics.

"My first cake creations were horrible. But my husband kept encouraging me to keep practicing. That's what it took. Keep repeating the techniques and eventually you improve."

And improve they did. Two months and three practice cakes after the Michaels course, Hill's transition into the business world came about on bunco night. "I brought a cake shaped and decorated like dice to my regular bunco night with the girlfriends. They loved it and I had three birthday cake orders by the end of the night." These first cake orders fell into the "practicing for friends" category. After about a year, Hill realized she had consistent orders and moved to a commercial facility, renting a local licensed church kitchen.

"For a small starter business like mine, renting a kitchen didn't go well. I didn't have that many orders yet, and the rental fees kept eating away at my profits," explains Hill, who ended up renting the kitchen for eight months. "My home kitchen is not only convenient, but spotless. I started thinking, why can't I bake at home?"

That insight led Hill to learn more about the cottage food movement nationally. She called her representative about introducing such a bill in Washington. While her representative offered support, her call, unfortunately, came too late in the legislative season for a bill to be introduced. But by sugar-coated serendipity, it turned out that just the day prior, a different representative had introduced a cottage food baking bill that was already in the legislative system. Hill jumped on this opportunity, helping champion and support the bill through to final passage in 2011. Hill even stood by Governor Christine Gregoire as she signed Washington's Cottage Food Operations Law into effect.

Unfortunately, it took another year for all the rules and regulations around this law to be worked out. "The law was supposed to take effect ninety days after signing, but our department of agriculture kept getting bogged down in the details. They lacked a budget to make it happen, too."

After making numerous phone calls, Hill eventually stepped in, showing up at the agency office in person and volunteering her time to keep the administration process going.

"I did a lot of the legwork for our department of agriculture, such as supplying them with several application templates from other states and creating a 'Frequently Asked Questions' sheet," explains Hill. She also supplied feedback and created a website and Facebook page for Washington's cottage food law, which she still maintains. "I brought the perspective of the cottage food law entrepreneur into the process and could ask the right questions so that the rules and regulations wouldn't stifle us."

On the day before July 4, 2012, everything changed for Hill. You might call it "Baking Independence Day." Hill officially received the first cottage food permit that gave the green light for her business to launch. Hill specializes in allergen-free cakes, with no dairy, tree nuts, gluten, eggs or soy. Her bakery is the only peanut-free kitchen in the Vancouver area, where nearly half of her cake orders are allergen-free.

"I love a challenge, and when a customer asks 'Can you make something,' I'll always say yes," Hill shares. This key customer service skill stems from her ability to listen deeply and hear what a potential client asks for. She has an open discussion with every customer, so what she delivers reflects the vision in their mind. It's not what you want but what the customer wants that matters. As it turns out, the diversity and challenges that come

Felicia Hill with a selection of her decorated cakes. Courtesy of FH Cakes

with new designs added to Hill's satisfaction and enjoyment in operating her business.

"My cake-decorating training came from watching YouTube videos while nursing my second son. There are so many resources out there with cake artists eagerly sharing their tips and techniques." She also recommends joining Cake Central (cakecentral.com), an online community for cake decorators. After watching techniques, Hill advises to simply practice until you nail it. Today, she loves creating unusual shapes and experimenting with three-dimensional cake designs, such as boats.

Pricing her products initially posed a challenge for Hill. "Looking back, when I started I undersold badly because I thought I needed to charge less because I wasn't as 'good' as other, more experienced cake decorators," Hill recalls. "I quickly learned that I needed to make a profit if this was going to be a real business and not just a hobby. You have to remember to pay yourself."

Hill researched online what others were charging and now has a $75 minimum order, with an average sale price of $125 for a small, two-tier cake. More intricate, three-dimensional cakes run around $250, since so much more time goes into making them.

"With cakes, you definitely want to get a website to showcase photos of your work. People want to visually see what you can do," advises Hill. Word-of-mouth referrals from satisfied customers remain her best advertising. Hill delivers most of her cakes directly, purchasing inexpensive corrugated brown cardboard moving boxes to transport her designs safely.

"My biggest recommendation for folks starting out is, don't give up," Hill offers. "I told myself, if I didn't start turning a profit in three years, I'd shut down, and, sure enough, it took till Year Three to start making money." Today she averages ten custom cakes a month with a strong repeat clientele. "I don't want to open a commercial bakery. I love the convenience of being right at home with my family."

One barrier Hill has encountered is the $15,000 gross sales cap stipulated in Washington's law. Thanks to her legislative experience, she is looking to the next legislative session to introduce an amendment to the law that increases the sales cap.

(5) *Get It in Writing*

Make hard copies of key pages off your state's website to document the cottage food law in case you're ever questioned. Just because your state has a law doesn't mean every state employee, farmers' market manager or even your local bakery business understands the particulars. You may find you have to educate others — or defend yourself — about what it is that you're doing. Websites are inherently dynamic; they're always changing. Create a paper trail and cover yourself.

If you have specific questions on the law as it applies to your business, your best bet is to e-mail the state contact off your state's cottage food page and receive an answer in writing (again, keep a hard copy). This covers you if there are questions in the future, particularly if these relate to what you can and can't do under the legislation.

For example, if you're not sure if a particular product qualifies, send the recipe and receive and document a specific reply. Give this process time. The day before your market is not a good time to call. Even if you need to make a phone call to prompt a reply, get a confirmation via e-mail as well. If you have a discussion with a state representative on the phone, one way to secure a reply is to send them an e-mail outlining what you discussed and the direction you received; then ask him or her to just reply, confirming that you're on the same page.

Remember two things as you navigate your state's law: responsibility and perspective. You're the one ultimately responsible for an accurate interpretation of the law, to the best of your ability. We add "your ability" since you need to feel confident that you have fully researched the legislation and asked enough questions to know that you can sell focaccia or cake pops in your state. Don't expect everything to be crystal clear or black and white; you may find yourself with varying views from different sources in your state capitol. Do your due diligence and then proceed.

Cake pops can be a delicious and unique way to celebrate a special event, or a easy and portable single serving item for a bake sale. John D. Ivanko

Secondly, carry a savvy businessperson's perspective. You're in charge of the cottage food law process. Sure, dealing with bureaucratic agencies and legislation can feel daunting or intimidating. But remind yourself that these often overworked government workers represent institutions that are supposed to be serving you; their salaries are funded by your tax dollars. State agencies serve you, and if you have a less than ideal experience with those administering the cottage food law, make your voice heard. Your opinion and suggestions might improve the path for the next food entrepreneur and may even spark legislative change.

Lobbying for or Amending a Cottage Food Law

If you live in a state with no cottage food law, don't cave in and give up in despair. Every cottage food law passed in the last decade has resulted from an initial individual citizen organizing others in their state to come together to get the bill passed, with the help of the state representative who sponsored or co-sponsored the bills.

Likewise, if your state law is limited — if, say, you want to sell cookies but your current law only allows you to sell high-acid pickles and preserves — then you too will need to take democracy by the horns and advocate, lobby and amend an existing cottage food law to include such items. Or, depending on your state's legislative protocol, this expansion may require a full new cottage food law.

Whatever your goal, make sure you have these three elements in your toolkit before diving into the democracy pool:

1. Partnerships

Consider collaboration the yeast that rises to the occasion and brings cottage food legislative change to life. We home cooks harbor business dreams and kitchen expertise, but we lack the deep pockets and big checkbooks others might have to influence politicians. Therefore, we need numbers. Numbers of people, people who vote. We need to demonstrate to our elected representatives the strong and widespread interest in cottage food law and the positive entrepreneurial impact it will have on our state's economy.

Some key places to seek partners include:

Your State Representatives

Your first call should be to your own representatives. In most states, this consists of two elected officials: one from the state senate and one from the state house of representatives, just like on the federal level. Whether or not you voted for them, these elected officials should be your most loyal champions, since you're their constituent.

You'll probably deal with your representative's aides and not him or her directly. Don't feel slighted. The legislator's staff forms the influential group that gets things done in that office. Staffers can also ☞

give you a snapshot of any pending cottage food legislation and other history, like past failed attempts at passing a similar bill. Your state representative most likely will have a small staff of a few people. The best option would be to connect with their chief of staff or the person who covers issues related to the department of agriculture or commerce.

Like-minded Organizations

Is there an existing statewide group that could adopt and champion your cause? This will help tremendously to provide both organizational strength as well as legitimacy to your proposed legislation. The more you can prove to representatives that the cottage food movement is a big deal with strong impact potential to your state's economy, the better your odds. Affiliating with a kindred-spirited non-profit group will help.

This will often be a sustainable agriculture advocacy group, since cottage food fits their mission of supporting family farms. Such an organization may also bring experience in the lobbying front and have a policy or government relation's person on staff to assist and advise. The Illinois Stewardship Alliance helped shepherd cottage food legislation in that state and we've partnered with the Wisconsin Farmers Union in our efforts to expand cottage food law in our state to include baked goods and increase the sales cap.

Potential Cottage Food Entrepreneurs

The pulse of your plan for cottage food law change comes from others just like you: fledgling food entrepreneurs who need this legislation to bring their kitchen business dreams to life. Do a thorough check to see if anyone is already organizing in your state and join forces. Start a Facebook page or webpage to connect and keep an e-mail contact list to get information out in a timely manner, especially when the bill is up for a vote and you need volumes of calls urging support to representatives across the state.

2. Plan

When you gather these partners, particularly your state representatives and kindred organizations savvy in the legislative process, get an immediate sense of the legislative schedule and how your proposed bill fits in. Most state governments operate under a fairly tight and specific schedule dictating when they meet for a vote and approximately how long it takes to shepherd a bill through the vetting process beforehand.

This vetting process often includes committee meetings where the bill is discussed and the pubic is invited to provide testimony. Of particular importance, these committee meetings provide an opportunity to organize supporters who, with their oral and written testimony, influence the committee to support the bill. If the committee does vote for it, the bill then moves to a full vote in either the state assembly or senate. Cue the Schoolhouse Rock song for a review of how your bill will become a law.

3. Patience

Realize your state legislature might only meet once or twice a year to vote on bills. If your bill doesn't make it through committee in time, it may have to wait a year, only to start the process all over again. The ☞

Wisconsin "Cookie Bill" cookie, baked and decorated by Shannon Heupel of Artfully Delicious Cookies.
JOHN D. IVANKO

democratic process can really drag. Occasionally, however, bills are "fast-tracked," usually (in our experience) because the process has been greased by outside campaign donations, political maneuvering or other monetary influences.

The cottage food movement by its very nature does not have big lobbying bucks or deep pockets behind it, so it may creep along like a glacier. We can foster patience and determination while simultaneously advocating and championing the grassroots, people-driven story. Get your inspiring tales of food businesses that such legislation would jumpstart out to the media. Write an op-ed for your local or state newspaper, a sample of which is featured on this book's website (homemadeforsale.com).

Apply a supersize dose of patience if your proposed legislation fails. Ready yourself for a good fight on the next round. In Wisconsin, for example, we learned this lesson well when advocating for a "Cookie Bill," proposed legislation to expand our cottage food law to include baked goods and increase the gross sales cap. Despite the fact that our bill received strong bipartisan support throughout the legislative process, passing committees and the full senate unanimously, it did not get onto the agenda for a vote on the assembly floor in the final round. By failing to put it up for a vote, the speaker of the house, who unilaterally sets the voting agenda, used his political position to effectively kill the bill for another year by omitting it from the agenda during the last session.

A blessing in disguise? Regrouping and plotting our strategy to reintroduce the bill next year, we'll be aiming even higher by increasing the gross sales cap and including greater product opportunities more in line with other states' cottage food laws. As they say, it's never over until it's over.

2

What's Cooking?

YOU MAY LOVE TO BAKE, can or cook up a storm in the kitchen. That's a great foundation for a cottage food enterprise. But there are a few steps to go through, transitioning from being a "home cook" to being a "food entrepreneur." This chapter examines some of your options and opportunities as a CFO, defined by the cottage food law where you live.

Cottage food laws vary a lot by state. The reason for this current patchwork of laws dates back to one of the underlying principles our country was founded upon: states' rights. In the US, the founding fathers believed in giving independence and governing authority to the states on many issues.

The way that works today regarding food is the US Food and Drug Administration (FDA) publishes the Food Code, a model for the states to base their food regulation on — all 700-plus pages of it. The Food Code provides a scientifically sound technical and legal basis for the food industry as a whole, and states generally abide by it. Another way to look at this is to think of state regulations as cars: there are lots of makes and models, but everything is pretty much the same under the hood. Because cottage food laws don't cross state lines, only concern yourself with what's required in your state. That's simple enough, right?

There are four key questions you need answered in your state's cottage food law before you get started:

- What products can you sell?
- Where can you sell your products?
- How are you allowed to sell your products?
- How much can you sell of your products?

Once you've answered these questions and understand how the cottage food law operates in your state, you'll then need to figure out whether what you love to make is worth selling. If people are clamoring for your pretzels, that's an excellent sign. In the end, your ability to sell products is based on creating items your customers want, need and are willing to buy at a fair price that they, not you, determine. That's where marketing — covered in several chapters of this book — comes in.

Question 1: What Products Can You Sell?

There's a reason for you to first see what types of products you can produce under your state's cottage food law. It's the classic glass-half-full versus glass-half-empty scenario: focus on what you can legally make and don't waste time, energy and money spinning your wheels on what you can't. Don't complain, just cook.

Your state's legislation will specifically outline those "non-hazardous" food items you can produce under cottage food law. In the simplest terms, the conventions used to define such food are low-moisture and high-acid. Sometimes the legislation will itemize what you can or can't sell.

Non-hazardous is the key word. You don't see that term used in recipes, right? By scientific definition, it refers to an item, usually a baked good, that has a low moisture level, measured as a water activity value of 0.85 or less. Or it can be a high-acid food, measured by an equilibrium pH value of 4.6 or lower. Some state legislation includes this exact verbiage about moisture levels and pH values. Your state may also define other non-hazardous food items you're welcome to sell.

The two types of foods most widely approved under cottage food laws are low-moisture baked goods and high-acid canned foods like pickles or preserves, each explored next.

Baked Goods

Nearly every state that has cottage food legislation on the books includes baked goods, so this is probably the most accessible category for launching your business. Baked goods are so prevalent in cottage food legislation because it's hard to mess up a loaf of bread or a chocolate chip cookie from a food safety perspective. Politicians, if nothing else, are mostly risk-adverse and conservative. Freshly baked, non-hazardous baked goods are in a different food "safety zone" than something like canned green beans, a low-acid canned item you'll never see on an approved list.

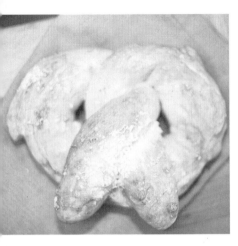

Fresh-baked pretzels can be a hit, especially if you make your own high-acid mustard to go with them. JOHN D. IVANKO

"While everyone from the media to Capitol Hill keeps spinning wheels trying to find the perfect panacea for job creation, especially in rural areas, they really need to look no further than our nation's kitchens. Our American history has roots in this idea of cottage businesses, from the butcher to the baker and other food artisans who create things at home that service their local community."

— PATTY CANTRELL, FOUNDER OF REGIONAL FOOD SOLUTIONS LLC

A simple way to understand non-hazardous baked goods is by asking this question: Does your item require refrigeration? If, like a custard pie, it does, then you can't sell it in nearly all states with cottage food laws.

Some common examples of items you can bake and sell to the public:

- Bread loaves
- Muffins
- Cookies
- Biscuits
- Crackers

Pumpkin bread, baked with pumpkins grown on-site. John D. Ivanko

Your items do, in fact, need to be baked to qualify as baked goods. Obvious, eh? But this also means you can't just combine items such as rolled oats, nuts and peanut butter to make an energy bar or trail mix. Nor can you add an ingredient to something already baked, like dipping graham crackers in chocolate. Depending on your state, these types of products may be covered separately in other categories (read on!), but they wouldn't be defined as a baked goods type product that has to meet the low moisture level requirement.

Missing from the approved non-hazardous baked goods list are any items filled with something that needs refrigeration. Moist fillings increase the moisture level and thereby increase the potential for harmful bacteria to thrive. There are a lot of variations on what a "filled" baked good can mean. Again, some

"I started my cookie business in 2008, from my home with eight hundred dollars. By my second year, I barely broke even. My business nearly quadrupled during my third year, bringing me from approximately 7 to about 28 orders per week. And last year, I averaged about 47 orders per week. Admittedly, I am an optimist, but if you had told me ten years ago that I would be able to build a cookie business from my home, doing what I am absolutely passionate about and grossing six figures into my fifth year in business, I would have certainly told you, 'You are NUTS!'"

— Aymee VanDyke, also known as Cookiepreneur and owner of Wacky Cookies, Virginia (wackycookies.com)

"There is so much untapped business opportunity to showcase each state's baking heritage; in Wisconsin we have everything from from Swiss bratzeli cookies to Norwegian lefse to a multitude of other cultural specialties. In my work chronicling the state's culinary legacy, I've meet many amazing home bakers who carry on Wisconsin food traditions. However, many of their baked goods can't be mass produced, and therefore you can't purchase them anywhere."

— TERESE ALLEN, WISCONSIN'S LEADING FOOD AUTHORITY AND HISTORIAN

states give specific guidelines while others may require you to contact the agency for clarification. A basic sugar frosting filling made with sugar, water and butter should be fine, but add in other refrigerated ingredients, such as cream cheese, and you'll likely be out of luck.

High-Acid Canned Goods (Preserves, Pickles and Salsa)

Second to baked goods, many cottage food laws permit high-acid

Low Moisture Means Baked Goods that are Safe

Don't panic if you see a slew of technical detail and numbers in your state's law defining non-hazardous baked goods. You don't need to be a scientist; you do need to ensure the baked product for sale is safe by following your state's guidelines. These definitions generally follow the FDA's Food Code of a "water activity value of 0.85 or less."

These definitions describe baked goods with a low moisture content, which inhibits mold growth and means they can be kept at room temperature. They're shelf-stable. If an item is too moist, pathogens — the bad bacteria that can cause disease — grow. In such cases, these items need to be refrigerated to prevent the growth of harmful bacteria. The lower the water activity level number, the drier the food item and therefore the safer it is, because it is less prone to bacteria growth.

A state's law may list specifically what is allowed, such as breads and cookies, and what is not, like cream pies or churros that contain a moist filling. Anything made with meat is always a definite no. What about frostings? A traditional butter cream frosting would be too moist to qualify, but some non-hazardous recipes exist that involve frosting made with a vegetable shortening base.

If you have a specific recipe you want to make and sell and are unsure where it fits on the water activity scale, your best first step is to e-mail it to the state agency administering your cottage food law. If they're unsure, the agency may ask you to conduct an official water test, which involves sending a sample to a professional laboratory for analysis. There is no universal definition of what baked goods qualify under cottage food laws.

canned items made in home kitchens. The "high-acid" refers to fruits and vegetables that are either naturally high in acid, such as tomatoes, or that become acidified through pickling or fermenting. To be considered high-acid, these products must have an equilibrium pH of 4.6 or less. If your memory of tenth-grade science is a bit hazy, this pH number measures acidity; the lower the number, the more acidic the food item.

Examples of high-acid canned products include:

- Jams and jellies
- Salsa
- Chutneys
- Pickled vegetables and fruits
- Sauerkraut
- Kimche
- Applesauce

Jars of Slow Jams jam (facebook.com/ slowjamsjam), handcrafted and featuring Michigan produce and sugar. Based in Grosse Pointe, Michigan, the business was originally started under cottage food legislation by Shannon Byrne.
John D. Ivanko

Cottage food laws only refer to canned items processed with university extension-approved methods such as a hot water bath. High-acid items that don't qualify in the legislation are refrigerator pickles or pickles made in a crock. Again, for the purposes of nearly all cottage food laws, if your product requires refrigeration, you can't sell it.

Unlike water activity level, pH can be measured at home if permitted by your state. You can use a pH meter, which needs to be properly calibrated on the day it is used. More common are paper pH test strips, also known as litmus paper; you simply dip these in a sample jar, and the color will turn based on the acidity level and related pH number. Paper strips work best if a product has a pH of 4.0 or less; the strip's range should go up to a pH of 4.6. Depending on your state's rules, you may need to do a pH test on each batch or over a state-defined time frame. While more pricey, a pH meter can provide a more exacting measurement of acidity.

Canning and creating high-acid products are very different processes than baking. Canned items, whether high-acid or not, are more science than culinary art. While you can alter, experiment with and personalize your biscotti recipe until it is uniquely your own, this isn't the case with canning recipes. At best, you'll be able to adjust your spices and ratios of vegetables.

There are plenty of university extension-sanctioned recipes that have been thoroughly tested, from classic items like basic strawberry jam to more modern delicacies such as garden chutney and sweet pepper relish. Some states allow specific canning recipes from sources like the current edition of the *Ball Blue Book Guide to Preserving*. But note that just because a recipe is in a canning cookbook doesn't mean it will qualify under the state law. Just follow the state-mandated recipes and protocol, and you're good to go.

What if you want to use your great-grandma's special family recipe for blackberry preserves? Some states will allow you to alter and create your

Building Your High-Acid Knowledge Base

While home canning goes back generations, remember it's a traditional art that has become safer over time thanks to our increasing scientific understanding of the process. Great-grandma's tomato sauce recipe based on yesterday's practices — which often did not include adequate water bath times or sanitation procedures — could potentially do more harm than good. So stick with current recipes from reliable and state-approved sources.

Another reason to steer clear of old recipes: some of the vegetables used today have changed in composition. Garden tomatoes, for example, have been bred to become less acidic to appease our taste preferences, a change that could significantly alter the results of the canning process and, therefore, the safety of grandma's original recipe.

So go through a reputable source for high-acid canned recipes, such as:

- *Ball Blue Book Guide to Preserving,* by Alltrista Consumer Products (current edition)
- *Ball Complete Book of Home Preserving*, edited by Judi Kingry and Lauren Devine (current edition)
- Cooperative Extension Offices in US: csrees.usda. gov/extension
- Home Food Preservation from Penn State University: foodsafety.psu.edu/preserve.html
- National Center for Home Food Preservation: nchfp. uga.edu
- The National Center for Home Food Preservation offers a free, self-paced online course, "Preserving Food at Home: A Self-Study," for those who want to learn more about home canning.

Profile

Beginning Farmer Pickles Profits

Dedicated to growing food sustainably and building community, Erin Schneider and her husband, Rob McClure, own Hilltop Community Farm, a small-scale diversified community supported agriculture (CSA) farm and orchard in LaValle, Wisconsin. Exemplifying how beginning farmers can use cottage food laws, they've increased and diversified their farm income one home-filled canning jar at a time.

"Thanks to our state's cottage food law covering high-acid foods, I was able to quickly and easily increase and diversify my farm income stream," explains Schneider. We generate more than two thousand dollars annually by selling sweet pickle relish, salsas and jams at local farmers' markets and community events."

Not only did Schneider increase her farm income, these value-added goods showcase the farm's fruits and vegetables in new ways and put any surplus to profitable use. "Every farmer or gardener ends up with a lot of extra something at the end of a harvest," Schneider laments. "You could give it away or add it to the compost pile. Why not make some extra money off the labor you already invested?"

Schneider focuses on recipes that showcase their farm's bounty and specialty items, such as jam made from black and red currants. Along with classic pickle recipes — dill, bread and butter and relish — she makes tomato-based red salsa and salsa verde, a green sauce made with tomatillos, all appealing to the spicy crowd. The jars retail between five dollars for a four-ounce jam jar to eight dollars for a pickle quart, with volume discounts of 5 percent off purchases over thirty dollars.

Schneider has two primary sales outlets:

- **Direct orders from CSA members**
  Hilltop Community Farm gives their CSA members an order form for her

Name: Erin Schneider and Rob McClure

Business: Hilltop Community Farm (LaValle, Wisconsin)

Website: hilltopcommunityfarm.org

Products: sweet pickle relish, salsa and jam made with farm-grown produce

Sales venues: winter holiday market, community supported agriculture (CSA) shares, member sales

Annual sales: $2,000

Erin Schneider in front of her farm stand that features her jam, salsa, sweet pickle relish made from her farm-grown produce.
COURTESY OF HILLTOP COMMUNITY FARM

relish, salsas and jams so they can stock up and easily add it to their weekly delivery.

"Producing and selling these canned goods is a win-win for us: we have an added income source that keeps us diversified, and it helps support our bigger mission of helping our members and community eat seasonally year-round."

- **Winter holiday market**

Schneider and McClure attend one key holiday market to sell their canned items, the Fair Trade Holiday Festival each December in Madison, Wisconsin. The gathering attracts an affluent, gift-giving crowd supportive of local agriculture. Best of all: it's the holidays and everyone comes wanting to shop and spend.

Erin Schneider selling at the Fair Trade Holiday Festival in Madison, Wisconsin.
COURTESY OF HILLTOP COMMUNITY FARM

"It's a super busy day, but this is a prime sales venue for us where we usually sell over 120 jars and can gross over six hundred dollars at one market. The folks coming are perfectly on-target for buying what we're making." Booth fees for these types of venues range from fifty to a hundred dollars.

"Bundling similar items together as a suggested gift package helps move sales," recommends Schneider. She groups similar pickled items as a "spicy sampler" and clusters the colors of the jars together on the display table in ways that place complementary colors alongside each other.

Schneider discovered that sampling plays a key role in closing the sale and garnering a premium price for her products, especially for some of her more unusual fruits like currants. "If people can taste something, I find they will spend up to two dollars more per jar because they feel confident in what they buy." Her recipes come from family classics like her grandma's relish, making sure all the pH levels and processing procedures are accurate by today's modern standards.

Such high-acid canned food ventures come with a distinct seasonal work schedule: lots of processing time during peak summer, especially if you grow and harvest your own fruits and vegetables, but then your labor completely ends and you only need to sell your inventory. Schneider advises beginning business start-ups to practice recipes in small batches until they perfect their canning technique.

"It takes us about one day a week from about mid-July through September to process our lines of canned products. This can add up to some long summer days," Schneider explains. "It takes two to four hours to harvest the produce. Then we'll crank in the kitchen for about six hours at night." An organized kitchen helps tremendously, developing a system for organizing and sterilizing all their equipment.

"There's always a couple of weeks of summer harvest overload when we need to get things processed right away, but a perk is quality family bonding time in the kitchen," laughs Schneider. Her mom will come over and help chop produce, and husband McClure holds the title of Resident Pickle Master. "Who needs date night when you can hang out over a steamy water bath canner together?"

Erin Schneider teaching a canning workshop at the Reedsburg Fermentation Fest: A Live Culture Convergence in Reedsburg, Wisconsin.
Courtesy of Hilltop Community Farm

own recipes after you complete the Master Food Preserver course. This is similar in format to the Master Gardeners program, also through university extension. There seems to be a revival with this new home-canning movement. The Master Food Preserver is a one-day intensive class that goes into the nitty-gritty science of pH and food safety procedures. Like the Master Gardeners, once you complete it, you can serve as a community education resource for local folks with canning questions.

Mixed Bag: Other Possible Cottage Food Products

Depending on your state, you may have an additional, mixed bag of products you can sell that may include dried mixes, herbal blends, chocolates, butters, condiments, dried pasta, roasted products — even cotton candy! There's no rhyme or reason to the list. Some of the items could just be things some person in that state really wanted to make in their home kitchen to sell to the public. Don't be surprised if your state allows one product while a neighboring state does not.

Check your state laws to see if any of the following items are possible:

- Candy, such as brittle and toffee
- Chocolate-covered nonperishable foods, such as nuts and dried fruit
- Chocolate-covered pretzels, marshmallows, Rice Krispie treats and graham crackers
- Cotton candy
- Dried fruit
- Dried pasta
- Dry baking mixes
- Granola, cereals and trail mixes
- Herb blends and dried mole paste
- Honey and sweet sorghum syrup
- Nut mixes and nut butters
- Popcorn
- Vinegar and mustard
- Roasted coffee
- Dried tea and dried tea blends
- Waffle cones and *pizelles*

Rice Krispies "sandwiches" sold at the International Chocolate Festival at the Fairchild Tropical Botanic Garden in Coral Gables, Florida. JOHN D. IVANKO

Handmade chocolates sold at the International Chocolate Festival at the Fairchild Tropical Botanic Garden in Coral Gables, Florida. John D. Ivanko

Question 2: Where Can You Sell Your Products?

Each cottage food law will dictate where you can sell your product directly to the public. In Montana and Nebraska currently, two of the states with the most restrictive cottage food laws, you can only sell your approved products at a farmers' market. That's it.

Even if your state's law allows sales at a farmers' market, that doesn't mean this venue must allow you to sell there. Some farmers' markets have bylaws or rules that exclude cottage food enterprises. For example, the Dane County Farmers' Market held in Madison, Wisconsin — one of the largest in the nation — requires that canned products be made in a licensed commercial kitchen.

Many states, however, offer a lot more flexibility in terms of the sales venues. The more options the better, in terms of reaching potential customers. The states with the greatest sales venue options often include direct delivery, home pickup and mail order.

Question 3: How Are You Allowed to Sell Your Products?

Regardless of the state, all cottage food laws permit direct sales to the public. Some of the more restrictive states, however, only allow sales that are direct-to-customer. Read: no indirect sales to other businesses that resell your product. But in more than a dozen states, products can be sold through indirect or wholesale channels, to restaurants, specialty food shops, the local food cooperative or even Whole Foods Market.

If, or when, the time comes to scale up and turn your micro-enterprise into a macro-business and offer your products through a wider assortment of channels than are permitted by your cottage food law, you may have to rent a licensed food production facility, or build a second on-site, commercial kitchen if allowed in your state. Expanding along a continuum, your business may either scale up modestly to serve a few small retailers or become an all-hands-on-deck, full-time endeavor with employees, production in a commercially licensed facility, huge financial demands and plenty of governmental red tape to keep you busy seven days a week. At that point, it's no longer for a casual baker or pickle-maker.

Under no circumstances are you ever "catering." Cottage food laws do not permit food service. You may deliver your products to a customer, but not display or serve them. You can produce certain foods in your home kitchen and have them consumed off premises — just don't slice, plate or otherwise be involved in serving your product.

With rare exceptions, your cottage food-approved products must, in fact, be made in your home kitchen. If you decide to scale up to sell via indirect channels (covered in the final section of this book), you'll be renting a commercial kitchen somewhere or building one in your home. If in doubt, check the section of your state's law related to the "workplace."

Question 4: How Much Can You Sell of Your Products?

Most states have a gross sales cap on the products you're selling. This refers to the maximum gross sales your operations can reach per year, and range from $5,000 to $45,000. More than twelve states with cottage food laws allow unlimited sales with no gross sales caps.

What Products do You Want to Sell, and Which are Worth Selling?

Now that you have an idea of what you can legally sell in your state, what can you make that's worth selling?

Here's where the fun starts with testing out your food product ideas. If you already have a popular product, at least with the in-laws and co-workers, then jump to the next chapter and proceed. Otherwise you'll need to sort out some details, including determining your products, checking your recipes and figuring out your market niche. As we'll cover in the forthcoming marketing chapters, these considerations play an important role in the story about your product and business.

Product Selection

At this stage of your evaluation, what products did you have in mind? There are several approaches you might take to selecting your product.

- **Ingredients:** are the ingredients or products going to be organic, made with whole grain, kosher, allergen-free, without preservatives or artificial ingredients or gluten-free?
- **Recipe focused:** are the recipes unique or rare family recipes that are popular with family and friends? Is the recipe an all-from-scratch item or do you take shortcuts with pre-made crusts or fillings? Is your focus on ethnic cuisine, cultural food items or a seasonal specialty item?
- **Sourcing of ingredients:** will your products come from your neighbor's fruit trees, your backyard, farmers' market, the supermarket, Costco? How local are your local ingredients? Depending on your products, some of the ingredients may come from a combination of these sources.

Market Niche

When you break down your ingredient list, what most of us are selling is nothing more than the following:

- **Pickles:** cucumbers, plus vinegar, salt, sugar and spices
- **Bread:** flour, salt, yeast and water
- **Preserves:** fruit, sugar and water
- **Cupcakes:** sugar, butter, eggs, flour

In many cases, there may be similar products available where you live. What makes yours different — and better? In some cases, if your ingredients are from a neighbor's fruit trees, a cherished ethnic recipe passed down several generations or a unique product you've developed and perfected yourself, these may be reason enough for a successful launch in your neighborhood. A market niche is a defined segment of a larger market

you've identified as a potentially financially rewarding opportunity; more on this in Chapter 4, when we dig in and define your product from a marketing perspective.

Follow the Trends

Your business might be small, but you can still take advantage of emerging food trends, creating products that target what shoppers currently seek. Some market niches to explore might be the following:

- **Gluten-free**

  Only 1 in 133 Americans are diagnosed with celiac disease, unable to tolerate gluten in their diet, according to the National Foundation for Celiac Awareness. But gluten-free appears to be the hot health trend with more than 30 percent of Americans claiming to avoid gluten, reveals the consumer research firm NPD Group. According to Mintel, another market research firm, the gluten-free product category will grow 48 percent from 2013 to 2015, reaching sales of $15.6 billion in 2016. Bakery items such as bread products, cookies and snacks hold the largest market share at nearly 24 percent.

- **Allergy-free**

  According to the Mayo Clinic, eight foods account for 90 percent of all food allergies, five of which are common in baked goods: peanuts, tree nuts, milk, eggs and wheat (soy, fish and shellfish also made the list). More of us are being diagnosed as lactose-intolerant, so consumption of milk and other dairy products is out.

- **Organic**

  Total organic sales in the United States continue to rise, up nearly 10 percent annually and growing from $1 billion in 1990 to more than $26 billion in 2010, according to the Organic Trade Association.

- **Local**

  Research from Sullivan Higdon & Sink's FoodThink, "A Fresh Look at Organic and Local" 2012, finds that "70 percent of consumers would like to know more about where food comes from." They found that local was hot: "The vast majority of consumers (79 percent) would like to buy more local food, and almost 6 in 10 (59%) consumers say it's important when buying food that it be locally sourced, grown or made." Additionally, the National Restaurant Association's 2014 Culinary Forecast included locally grown produce, hyper-local restaurant sourcing of fresh items and farm/estate branded products on their Top 10 Trends list.

- **Ethnic flavors**

  Does your own family heritage offer unique specialty items folks can't purchase elsewhere? Ethnic flavors continue to increase in popularity, particularly from Mexico and Latin American countries, according to the Flavor Forecast from McCormick & Co.

Recipe Testing

Getting the spices just right for your pumpkin cookies may involve plenty of trial and error, mixing and matching and lots of tasting. Besides taste and flavor, you'll want consistency, since you'll get a bad reputation quickly if the delicious muffins you made one week are too sweet or flavorless the following week. McDonald's has built its quick-service restaurant empire around this idea of consistency — anywhere on planet Earth. It may not be the healthiest food in the world, but their Big Mac tastes exactly the same in Monroe, Wisconsin, as it does in Moscow, Russia. Customers expect this.

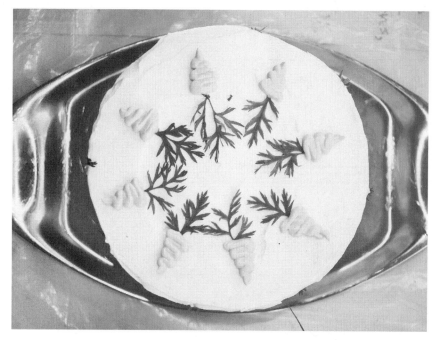

Carrot cake. John D. Ivanko

When you make your product with your recipe, does it turn out the same every time, day in and day out? Or does humidity, temperature or other factors create havoc with either your process or the ingredients?

Size is also an issue in consistency. Your cookies, bread or other baked items should be about the same size for the same price.

Product Testing

After nailing your recipes, it's time to test the product, since we're talking about something perishable. Your criteria might include taste, flavor, texture, shelf life (fresh, day old, best eaten fresh, longer term), labor involved, waste, space needs, speed of preparation and consistency.

It's important to have an honest and objective audience to help in your product testing. Are your pineapple salsa, pickled dilly beans or magical muffins as good as everyone says? Many people, as well-meaning as they may seem, will tell you what they think you want to hear. As you develop your products or product lines, it's important to find honest and objective testers who can provide practical feedback. Don't forget to "hire" your son or granddaughter as marketing consultants; kids can offer incredibly honest and fresh perspectives on your products and how they taste.

Product testing at this phase is different than completing a market feasibility study, where you examine a host of other variables, many having to do as much with marketing considerations and customer needs as taste. More on this in Chapter 9, after you've pulled together your ideas on marketing.

Authors' son Liam… savoring a sweet treat. Kids can be great taste-testers.
John D. Ivanko

3

Ideas in the Oven:
Identify Your Business Goals

BEFORE JUMPING INTO A BUSINESS, even a small, home kitchen-based one, you'll want to sort out your personal goals for the enterprise and set forth some realistic expectations. By default of the cottage food laws, your enterprise will not suddenly make you rich, though a few of you reading this book might discover a path to personal wealth based on a combination of your culinary ideas, talents and adept business decisions made along the way.

This chapter explores what it might mean to operate a business out of your home, helps you assess your current skills sets and talents and completes a few "quick checks" to make sure you don't put the food cart before the horse.

My Kitchen, My Rules

For many food entrepreneurs, one of the best parts of running your business is calling the shots. Everything is on your terms, within the parameters set forth by your state's cottage food law, of course. The law defines what you sell, how you sell it, to whom and when. You answer these questions yourself, perhaps with a little input from others you trust, respect and admire.

Before starting, however, you'll want to have a clear idea as to what you want to achieve with your business. Here are some of the many reasons CFOs open their operation:

- **Income to go out for a fancy dinner with your spouse or pay the bills**
  Thanks to the cottage food laws, created, in part, as a reaction to the recent trying economic times, turning a home kitchen into an income-generating profit center may allow you to splurge on a dinner out more often. Or it may be the difference between being able to pay the

bills or not. Most enterprises will never be a full-time endeavor; they can, however, add supplemental cash flow where it never existed before.

- **Enjoyment and fulfilling a dream passion**

When money is not the object, many people would choose to do something radically different than what they do now. They have a dream of being a baker, making canned preserves from a favorite family recipe or just running their own business. We started our Inn Serendipity Bed & Breakfast based on our vision; now we want to start a small bakery enterprise in our kitchen for the same reason.

Following your dreams and passion can be empowering, satisfying, enjoyable and meaningful in ways that no paycheck — even a big paycheck — could ever be. In the world of human psychology, such self-driven motivation is referred to as intrinsic. The extrinsic motivation for most jobs is money, a health insurance plan, a corner office or a gold watch; many of us have found that there never seem to be enough extrinsic rewards if you hate what you do or who you do it for.

- **Building community connections**

A hundred years ago, people were interconnected and interwoven in their community in ways no Facebook group could ever be. Their survival, in some ways, depended on the support, kindness and companionship of their neighbors. Citizens patronized their butcher, baker and candlestick maker, who in turn supported their business. Money recirculated in the community. The Made-in-China revolution sold by Wal-Mart and made possible by relatively cheap fossil fuels was a century away.

Now "cheap" energy isn't cheap any more, and food costs are rising faster than our incomes. Plus more of us are wondering just how what we eat is made and by whom, and questioning its safety. Some call this a food security issue. To reclaim our food supply, cottage food laws are expanding the reach to community supported farms, food cooperatives and farmers' markets, essaying a return — or at least a community option — to a time when we can buy from our neighbors again, legally.

- **Promoting local food**

We now have a name for someone who loves growing, eating and preserving food that's as close to home as possible: *locavore*. Thanks to

"I didn't want the 9-to-5 rat race. I wanted to do something I'd enjoy."

— ANGELA BROOKS-VAN NIEL, OF REDLANDS, CALIFORNIA, HOME-BASED OWNER OF SIMPLY FANCY CUISINE

A Food Network–inspired Baker

"I live with a bunch of foodies in my family who religiously watch the Food Network. We gave into the *Cupcake Wars* craze and started watching that show too," confesses Isa Lunsford of Lake Worth, Florida. Lunsford is no television-watching couch potato. While most viewers are content to live out their baking fantasies passively, Lunsford harnessed it as the inspiration to launch her business: "I can do that," she said, and the vision behind Sweet Pick Me Ups Bakery came to life in 2011.

As a lifelong baker, Lunsford came to the cottage food business table with a strong skill set in the kitchen — and business pragmatics. As a veteran certified public accountant (CPA) practicing for twelve years, she knows her way around income statements, balance sheets and complicated tax codes.

"While I never see my bakery as our family's sole source of income, I do understand and appreciate the fact that a business needs to be a smart investment," explains Lunsford. She set up Sweet Pick Me Ups Bakery as an LLC but chose to be taxed as an S corporation to create a liability shield between the business and her personal assets should any food safety or resulting lawsuit situation come up. The S corporation offered more asset protection and tax savings than a single-member LLC.

When she started Sweet Pick Me Ups in 2011, Lunsford still spent most of her time working in the debits and credits of the accounting world Monday through Thursday. But on Fridays, you found her baking for eight hours, selling a variety of items for a local farmers' market.

That schedule taught her two things. First, she realized she loved baking more than accounting. When her firm downsized in 2012, she had an opportunity to take an early retirement and jumped at the chance to devote more time to baking, leaving the stressful world of accounting behind. Second, while the farmers' market proved to be a great way to build name recognition and sample, the scene didn't add up to efficient, profitable sales, as she always ended up with things left over at the end of the day and found it hard to predict what would sell. Lunsford then decided the custom-order route worked better for her, focusing on direct, individual orders for specialty cakes, cupcakes and other bakery items. She could set her own schedule and never ended up eating leftover banana bread all week from the last market.

Name: Isa Lunsford

Business: Sweet Pick Me Ups Bakery LLC (Lake Worth, Florida)

Website: sweetpickmeups.com

Products: specialty custom-order cakes, cupcakes and cookies

Sales Venue: direct orders from customers

Annual Sales: $15,000

Lunsford taught herself how to create one-of-a-kind cakes with colorful fondant.
COURTESY OF ROSALIA SCALICI-BOU

"Today I mostly do fondant cakes in customized themes. That's where the demand is, and I love to keep my creative juices flowing," Lunsford says. She has earned a reputation for working with and delivering what a customer wants. Her cakes average two hundred dollars and she's willing to create things out-of-the-box for customers, such as flirty risqué cakes for bachelor and bachelorette parties in the shape of breasts or even Chippendale dancers. She found a wealth of tutorials with cake and fondant information online, as well as talking to seasoned bakers for additional tips. "There is always something to learn or a different way to do the same thing."

"I love creating new shapes and designs because I'm always learning something new," adds Lunsford. She improved her stacking of uneven cake shapes with practice over time and still finds dealing with Florida humidity a challenge. The icing can bubble and start to discolor. Cooling down the car prior to transporting the cake helps. For cookies, Lunsford recommends not bagging them until the last minute and also transporting in a cooled car.

Most of her business comes from referrals and word-of-mouth advertising. "I regularly post photos of my finished work to the website and Facebook page because this really helps folks visualize ideas and give me concrete direction in what they want."

"Challenges will come up and when they do, remember you always have alternatives and options," Lunsford advises. Living in a private community with a homeowners association, she realized the rules stated you could not conduct actual business transactions in your home with people stopping by. "I worked around this by simply delivering all my products. I build the delivery fee into my pricing along with any taxes. This works well with my customers as I keep things simple with one total cost for their order and no hidden extra charges." First-time customers get 10 percent off their order.

Not all people appreciate or are willing to pay a premium for her custom, high-quality products. "People sometimes expect the same pricing they'd pay at the local supermarket bakery. I now require 50 percent payment when placing an order to ensure commitment," Lunsford shares. She processes payment via check or uses Square for credit card processing.

"Setting my own hours and having flexibility to work around my family's schedules are priorities, so I've turned people away when things get too busy," Lunsford adds. Keeping things in balance and that fun factor high remain core priorities for her. "Remain small, fun and enjoyable, that's my advice."

Michael Pollan, author of *The Omnivore's Dilemma.* While he penned his tome from an ivory tower — in his case UC Berkeley, where fresh, local food is available year-round — this idea of local food appeals to any-one aware that what we find in most grocery stores and supermarkets today has more frequent flier miles than Warren Buffet. Thanks to the cottage food laws, as food entrepreneurs, we can close the local food loop with our value-added products, expanding the fresh selection of what's already available at more than eight thousand farmers' markets in the US.

- **Integrating family**
  Akin to fathers fishing with their sons or mothers baking cookies with their daughters, going into business with a spouse, sibling or the prover-bial Uncle Joe resonates in ways that no shopping excursion to the mall could ever do. Working with your family in a culinary operation provides a way to connect and build a relationship in an entirely new way. If you have older kids, what better way for them to learn about how to start a business and cook in the kitchen?

- **Needing a project**
  Perhaps the kids have fledged the nest, off to college or life as a young adult. Or maybe you're among the roughly seventy-five million retirees in America, looking for something to do besides another round of golf or cruise. There's no short-age of research that shows that staying active and engaged is an essential part of staying healthy. But sometimes we just need a project. Starting a small business built around a passion for cooking and favorite recipe can be exactly what the doctor might prescribe (if they weren't so focused on prescription drugs, that is). For some, a cottage food business can

Got Recipes?

What if you don't have any family recipes or personal favorites? Time to hit the cookbooks and Internet for ideas. Have fun with the research! Keep your receipts for your cookbooks and ingredients used for testing recipes; both can be legitimate "start-up" business expenses (a subject we cover in Chapter 12). You can also find a selection of recipes from our *Farmstead Chef* cookbook on the website for this book, including recipes for sugar cookies, crackers, pickles, jam, jelly, salsa and marmalade.

act as a drug, providing a life focus and fostering interactions with other people and their community.

The reason you open your business may be one of the above, or a combination of several. It's important not to lose sight of why you started, since everything may not go as planned. Life can toss us curveballs and open a few trapdoors when we least expect them. Our goal in writing this book is to help you steer a course that's true to your goals and guide you on your journey to success, however you define it, missing as many of these trapdoors as possible.

Recipe for Success

For many people, success has come to be defined by the size of their bank account, the square feet of their house or the profitability of their business. Too often, the quality of your product, the satisfaction of your career or your general level of happiness is trivialized or marginalized. It becomes an afterthought.

So when it comes to your cottage food business, how you define success will determine, to a large extent, whether you achieve it. Here are a few ways some food entrepreneurs have defined their success:

- Perfecting a great family recipe and sharing it with others;
- Creating a unique product;
- Celebrating a passion for cooking;
- Launching a small business and making a little profit, every year;
- Enabling someone with a food allergy to enjoy something they couldn't before;
- Being part of the celebratory process of a customer's special event, like a birthday party, wedding or fiftieth anniversary.

When you define what you mean by success, you've put it in your terms. This perspective will lend itself well to putting your ideas down on paper in the form of a simple plan. Plus it will help silence snarky people who drift into your life or deflect the negativism, criticism or cynicism you may encounter when you follow your dreams while others fail to realize theirs. Your vision, determination and perseverance will transform your intent and actions into success, on your terms.

CFO Self-assessment

Do you have what it takes to be a CFO, a cottage food operator? More than an idea, recipe or home kitchen filled with appliances, becoming a small food business owner will require a level of knowledge, skill and talent, each addressed below.

1. Food Knowledge

What's your culinary know-how? Having a degree in food science, years working at a bakery or a stint at a delicatessen would help you achieve the goals you've set for your business from the perspective of what you can accomplish in the kitchen. But don't underestimate the "on-the-job" experience of raising a family of four if you prepared most of the meals at home. Perhaps you're the legendary birthday cake maker of the family. Perhaps you already can enough food products to keep your family, friends and a few neighbors stocked up each winter. Every product you make reflects your cumulative knowledge of cooking skills, techniques, recipes and ingredient selection.

When deciding what products you want to make for sale, go with what you love and feel there's a market for. We'll cover the feasibility testing of

Intelligent Fast Failure: It's How We Learn What Works!

Civil and environmental professor and inventor Jack V. Matson, PhD, dedicates his life to practicing "intelligent fast failure," an expression he coined to capture the essence of innovation. It's captured in his irreverently titled book, *Innovate or Die: A Personal Perspective on the Art of Innovation.*

In his book, Matson suggests that the goal with intelligent fast failure is to move as quickly as possible from new ideas to new knowledge by making small and manageable mistakes — intelligent failures. By moving quickly, we can determine what works and what doesn't, without draining the bank account or the energy devoted to developing the idea. When you come out with new products, some will catch on and some will fail. While you may love the taste of pickled radishes, there many not be enough other people that do too. Cottage food enterprises fit perfectly into this fast-failure mode. Everything you do is small batch and experimental. Not sure which dry candy-combo harbors the most customer appeal? Make a tray of each and bring them all to market to see which sell best.

The key is to keep learning and try to avoid letting your intelligent fast failures negatively influence your emotions or self-esteem. And by all means, fail falling forward.

your product in Chapter 9. Do you love baking, making pickles or mixing spices together? Is kneading dough a passion, or something you procrastinate doing? Would a call for a large-batch production of fifteen dozen muffins for a corporate retreat be stressful or a fun challenge?

Culinary Training

When arriving at the burgeoning cottage food industry, you may be drawn by an interest in learning a new craft or doing something you've always wanted to do but just never had the chance to tackle. Until now.

If you need to pick up some skills or hone a few you already possess, a wide range of workshops offered by non-profit or private for-profit organizations and university or community college-level courses could get you chopping, dicing, canning and baking like a professional. From learning about artisan-style yeast-raised breads with recipes and techniques from around the world to cakes, cookies and pies, these programs may open your eyes to what might be possible in your kitchen.

Some states, eager to help get people to work, have created programs or resources to support new home cooks and their businesses. That's helpful, because these programs aren't cheap. Keep in mind, however, that you may be able to deduct these courses as a legitimate business expense; more on this in Chapter 12.

The following shortlist of programs designed to help people jump-start their culinary careers may be worth a look. Be mindful, however, of your goals and aspirations, perhaps avoiding those programs or degrees that might push you in the direction of working at a

restaurant, institutional kitchen or similar operation. A good question to ask: How many of their students go off to start their home-based food enterprise? For the most practical experience, avoid classes or workshops heavy on food samples and light on educational content. Remember, you're not a recreational or hobby baker or cook. You're operating a business.

- **Michaels**
  michaels.com
  This national arts and crafts store chain offers introductory through advanced decorating classes through the Wilton Method of Cake Decorating, covering cakes, cookies, cupcakes and brownies. Workshops often cover topics like gum paste and fondant flowers.

- **Chopping Block, Chicago**
  thechoppingblock.net
  Their "Boot Camps" dive into the fundamentals and nuances of the culinary arts, and reveal tricks of the trade. The challenge might be finding a course specific to your interests.

- **Williams-Sonoma**
  williams-sonoma.com
  Check out their free Technique Classes, hour-long sessions that focus on a specific culinary skill, sometimes with a seasonal theme, such as Easter ☛

baking. They also offer longer, fee-based cooking classes.

- **Sur La Table**
  surlatable.com
  Introductory hands-on classes showcase different dishes and techniques.

- **Food Craft Institute**
  foodcraftinstitute.org
  The Food Craft Institute, based in Oakland, California, works to create and improve the viability of small- and medium-scale value-added food businesses in rural and urban America. Courses combine classroom and hands-on education to teach traditional food-making techniques alongside the entrepreneurship skills needed to turn those skills into viable businesses.

- **The Culinary Institute of America (CIA)**
  enthusiasts.ciachef.edu
  With campuses in New York, California and Texas, the CIA offers culinary education programs in the form of "Boot Camps" designed around baking, pastry, specialty and hearth breads, and basic skills.

- **Carlos Bakery**
  carlosbakery.com
  How can you go wrong with hands-on cake decorating classes at Carlo's Bakery in Hoboken, New Jersey, or at other Carlo's Bakeries, owned by "Cake Boss" Buddy Valastro?

Be realistic and honest in your self-assessment, but don't sell yourself short when it comes to your cumulative knowledge. Experience is the best teacher of all. When your recipes turn out the same every time you make them, that's a good sign.

If you like the idea of being a home baker but struggle because your recipes don't turn out as tasty or look as attractive as they appear to be on the Food Network, recognize that you might want to learn some new skills (which can be fun, too) or cultivate your existing talents further. Practice really does make perfect. Many food entrepreneurs have spent months, if not an entire year, tweaking, modifying and perfecting their customized, decorated sugar cookies that they now sell for two to five dollars each.

Beyond the accredited and non-accredited programs, workshops and short courses, you may also pick up some quick experience in your area of interest by working at a bakery, restaurant or catering business. If you love baking but want to see how another company does it, consider working part-time for a while at bakery or one of those fancy cupcake-making places; you wouldn't be able to use their secret, proprietary recipes, but you could walk away with practical knowledge about the industry you want to break into.

Another way to get in some experience might be as a volunteer at your church for events that involve food preparation; maybe you could handle the dessert or bread baking and test out your recipes. A non-profit organization that regularly offers some food at their events could be another route to go. For example, our Monroe Arts Center in Wisconsin sets out various nibbles during all their gallery openings; this could be a place for us to try out recipes and garner feedback without spending a cent of our money.

Exercising your "mind muscle," repeating over and over again the techniques needed for kneading dough or twisting croissants, translates to a more consistent, higher-quality product. The more practice you put in, the better the results. According to Malcolm Gladwell's book *Outliers* and based on a study by Anders Ericsson, consider adopting the "10,000-hour rule," which states that it takes approximately this amount of focused practice time to perfect a skill. That's twenty years, practicing an hour and a half a day. For many of you home cooks, you're already there!

2. Business Knowledge

What other talents or attributes do you possess that can help drive your enterprise? Can you write well? Are you a people person or someone with a knack for selling? Do you never grow tired of social media, always chattering on Facebook or tweeting? Are you comfortable enough with software on your computer to make brochures, flyers, invoices and receipts?

While you may bake a blue-ribbon-winning torte for the state fair, how much of the business skills do you have to help propel your business along? Even on a small scale, any skills with planning, marketing and managing the financial aspects of your business can go a long way in helping you achieve your goals. The more you can do yourself, the less you will need to contract out for a graphic design service for your labels, a freelance editor to help write the copy describing your product, a designer for your website or a bookkeeper to manage the money.

3. General Knowledge or Talents

How strong are your community networks? Would it be easy to share what you're doing, word of mouth, and then sit back and start filling orders, or are your community connections more limited to church, school or place of employment? Are you an organized or tidy person? Both organizational skills and cleanliness are extremely valuable to any food enterprise. Can you manage multiple projects at the same time, or do you find you like to do things one at a time? While balancing your work and life, having the ability to multi-task may make operating a home-based business less overwhelming.

Now you've clarified your goals, completed a CFO self-assessment and gained a better understanding of what you might be in for. In the next section and a series of chapters on marketing, we'll turn your "half-baked" ideas and recipes into products ready for market.

Whatever you do, remember to savor what you create. It's okay to cut a piece of pie for yourself.
John D. Ivanko

Selling Your Story: Marketing

SECTION 2

4

Product Development: Design, Name, Logo and Packaging

AWIDE RANGE OF DIFFERENT ELEMENTS go into defining a great product, including the uniqueness of your recipe, the quality of the ingredients, the packaging, perhaps the specific process of its artisanal, small-batch production and, even, the messaging you've created around your product.

As we touched on earlier, marketing is a term that covers a wide range of considerations associated with selling your homemade item. Most business schools cover the 4 Ps of marketing: Product, Price, Place (how you distribute your item) and Promotion, both in the form of paid advertising and "free" public relations.

We explore three additional Ps in our *ECOpreneuring* book, in part because marketing has become so pervasive and integrated into day-to-day routines, often in subtle or clever ways. It permeates our life through product placement in movies, naming rights for stadiums or campus buildings, Facebook updates or reviews on Yelp. These additional 3 extra Ps of marketing — People, Partnerships and Purpose — reflect our values and belief systems and connect us to our community.

Because marketing plays such a pivotal role in the success of any product, we've broken the 7 Ps of marketing down into several chapters. Realize, however, that the most effective marketing efforts are those that combine all seven elements into one cohesive, integrated and clear plan that can be effectively implemented.

Niche, Target and Positioning

Before getting into the product aspect of marketing, we'll touch on three very important concepts first: finding your niche, defining your target market and positioning your product.

Finding a Niche with Potential

Nearly all food businesses, large and small, assess potential markets, carving out a niche that seems most likely to earn enough money by selling a product to make it worth pursuing. If you don't make some profit, at least three out of five years, you're not in business, according to the IRS; you're just a hobby. We'll cover this more in Chapter 12.

A niche is a segment of a broader market where you believe your product can do well. Because of your product's unique characteristics, better quality or because it faces little competition, you may find greater flexibility in terms of how you market and sell it. Remember, if you define your niche too narrowly, or if there aren't enough customers who want what you make at the price for which you're selling it, then this niche doesn't have the market potential to make your business viable. Don't throw in the towel, just re-evaluate your goals and examine ways to expand your market without being everything to everyone.

Defining Your Target Market

While a niche is often product-focused, your target market is the audience or potential customers you want to reach, serve and satisfy with your products. The 7 Ps of marketing are guided or defined by who you select as the target market. In other words, the customers most likely to purchase your products in a large enough quantity at the price you've determined will allow your business to prosper.

There are a number of ways you can define your target market:

- **By demographics:** age, gender, geography and income level, among many other variables
  Example: ages 30–40, female, living in Smalltown, New York, earning $50,000 to $100,000/year
- **By psychographics:** attitudes, beliefs and value systems
  Example: a Cultural Creative "locavore" who loves artisanal food products, especially those that are organic and made without preservatives. Different from Traditionals and Moderns, Cultural Creatives are more attuned to environmental and social issues.

You'll need to define and understand your customers in both demographic and psychographic ways. Think about it this way: demographics help you understand who your customers are while psychographics help determine why your customers buy what they do. Keep in mind that the needs of your customers may not even be real; they could just be perceived. In other words, your customers may not even know they need your product, even if they do. Think: impulse purchases. From this information, you can then develop your marketing strategy, and from that, a marketing plan that addresses those 7 Ps.

Due to your familiarity with and assessment of the marketplace, you may already have a solid grasp of who would buy your products. You'll probably start by selling to neighbors, family or friends already clamoring for your products. Maybe they attend the same church, work in the same office or school, serve in the same civic organizations or attend the same youth soccer games. This works great until you find yourself wanting to sell more products and ramp up your operations to reach customers beyond your immediate network. At that point, you'll need to flush out the target market more thoroughly if your marketing efforts are to be effective.

Positioning Your Product

In marketing jargon, the expression of differentiation is called positioning: the combination of marketing elements that go into defining your product. Defining exactly how your product might appeal to your customers in terms of their needs or desires and the benefits it provides can be tricky. While you may believe you have the most unique and tasty fruit-flavored graham crackers ever, in the end, your potential customers need to share this perception and feel that it meets their needs as a healthy snack (assuming that's one of the benefits of your product). Product development research and a market feasibility study, covered in Chapter 9, guide this process.

Positioning can consider all 7 Ps of marketing, plus how your product might be used or the solution to a problem it addresses. Often, positioning can involve a combination of several variables. For example, your sugar-free sweet rolls could be a solution as a breakfast item for customers seeking ways to cut back on their sugar. Or that same sugar-free roll could be a delicious and healthier way to savor a snack, perhaps with a cup or coffee or tea.

Keep in mind that there's a big difference between being product-focused and market-focused, especially if your aim might be to scale up your

"Homemade" is the buzzword that CFOs celebrate with authenticity and pride.
John D. Ivanko

operations. The market — your customers — are the ones telling you what they want, what benefits they perceive, what problem is being solved, or what needs are being met with your product. Are gluten-free breads absent in your community? Is a well-attended local arts show missing a food vendor, with hungry art shoppers with no place to go for a snack?

With positioning, you're conveying what your product is, how it's different from the competition and why a customer should buy it from you. One route to success may be to come up with a "signature" product, something unique. Perhaps it's your uncommonly good approach to a common recipe. Bonus points for being clever, creative or distinctive in describing it. Even when you have no competition for your product, its taste will ultimately determine whether customers come back for more.

What you're actually selling could be much more than just the taste, flavor, texture, size or appearance of your food product. If you package or distribute it as a gift for tourists or the holiday season, your approach will be far different than if it was a product offered at a farmers' market. Depending on your item, you may even offer some form of service, like a guarantee of satisfaction.

For example, a Swiss-style cookie sold in a Swiss community with lots of tourist traffic might be positioned as an edible gift or a souvenir. The name, packaging, price and label should aid in this by eliciting a clear and prompt "I should try this now!" thought in a potential customer's mind while they're browsing the arts and crafts fair where you've set up a small stand.

Price can appeal to a customer on a limited budget, or deter an upscale clientele who might happily pay a premium for an item with high-quality ingredients or fresh from the oven. For many impulse purchases, convenience, comfort or hunger may drive the exchange; customers may pay a premium for any one of these qualities. How your product is different can take interesting forms; perhaps you deliver by bicycle. For example, Domino's Pizza, the national pizza chain, is famously known for being in the delivery business, not the pizza business. That's how they do pizza different.

Depending on your marketing strategy, you may be able to create an entire experience around the enjoyment of your product and the love that went into making it. Starbucks sells an experience, not just coffee.

Who knew so many Americans would pay a lot of money to order a double tall skim vanilla latte and hang out in a coffee house instead of a bar. Starbucks identified a perceived need among people and delivers a "coffee

Ideas Everywhere

When exploring how to label, package, price and sell your products, there's nothing wrong with seeing how other food entrepreneurs do it. Wander the aisles of a Whole Foods Market or a specialty gift store that sells food products. Below are a few more places to check out:

- Specialty Food Association's Fancy Food Shows, held on both coasts every year, and their informative website (specialtyfood.com).
- Mother Earth News Fairs (motherearthnews.com/fair), with a focus on sustainable ingredients for a wide range of food products.
- igourmet.com — if you're looking for how other food artisans create gift baskets and design their labels, check out this online gourmet food and gift retailer.
- stonewallkitchen.com — another source of ideas and to see how a Maine company thrives in the specialty food business.
- Natural Products Expo, East and West, focus on natural, organic and healthy-lifestyle products (expowest.com and expoeast.com).
- Green Festivals, hosted by Green America and Global Exchange, are now the largest and longest-running sustainability and green living events held in various large cities throughout the US (greenfestivals.org), with an entire section devoted to specialty food products.
- Good Food Awards (goodfoodawards.org), organized by Seedling Projects, is the first national awards platform to recognize American craft food producers who excel in superior taste *and* sustainability. The awards for outstanding American food producers and the farmers who provide their ingredients are given out at a ceremony and marketplace at the Ferry Building in San Francisco. The eleven award categories are beer, charcuterie, cheese, chocolate, coffee, confections, pickles, preserve, spirits, oil and honey.
- National Restaurant Association Show (show.restaurant.org/Home) in Chicago, one of the world's largest food and beverage trade shows. While focused on food service, the NRA Show also reveals the latest culinary trends and new products.
- Good Food Festival and Conference (goodfoodfestivals.org) in Chicago links some of the best local farmers and family-owned producers of food and farm products with the public, trade buyers and leaders in the field to foster relationships that facilitate the growth of local food systems.
- Artisanal LA (artisanalla.com) in Los Angeles showcases the best artisanal food vendors from around the country, from bakers to chocolatiers, canners to coffee roasters.

experience" in a way that differentiates them from the hundreds of thousands of coffeehouses and cafes that already exist.

A supermarket now contains, on average, more than 42,000 products, according to the Food Marketing Institute. Our modern-day marketplace is about choices, providing something for everyone, with companies vying for market niches and every dollar of the consuming public's disposable income. With 70 percent of the US economy based on "consumer spending," your product is directly linked to this broader economy. Making a great-tasting product is only the start.

There's no "right" way to position your product; the choices are infinite. But if you're stuck with a bunch of unsold items at the end of the day, you'll need to re-evaluate both your product *and* your marketing efforts.

Product Design and Attributes

While largely guided by your state's cottage food law, there's plenty of breathing room for what you create in your kitchen to sell to the public. It's the combination of your ingredients and the packaging, presentation and pricing — plus the story you create around your product — that gives your product its identity or personality. How you define the attributes and aspects of your product help differentiate it from others in the marketplace.

There are, however, certain conventions used in the industry that you'll need to follow, since that's also what your customers are expecting. Size and quantity are two important considerations. If your muffins are double the size of others at a community event, are you sure you can charge double the price, or do you even need to? Alternatively, people are used to getting discounts when they buy extra. So consider having a sliding scale for items sold by the half and full dozen.

If you're like us, you may already have a few well-tested recipes for products that just need a plan for sharing them with those who want to buy them. Our chocolate biscotti crunch, chocolate-chip zucchini loaves and chocolate-chip pumpkin muffins may soon have an outlet, thanks to Wisconsin's pending Cookie Bill. Our distinguishing attributes are organic ingredients, many of which come from our organic farm, which is completely powered by the wind and sun. Following our concern for the environment, our packaging is made from recycled content and can be composted.

Naming Right

There is no right name for your product. But there are names that tend to elicit a smile, convey a mood or feeling, or are just plain fun. While the name you give it should be true to the product and reflect the ingredients

Tools for Product Creation

There are lots of tools used by inventors, entrepreneurs and people working in creative fields, most of which work perfectly for developing new food products. Here are a few you might want to try if you don't have Auntie Emma's secret recipe:

- **Brainstorming**

  Among the more common ways of coming up with creative ideas and solutions to problems, brainstorming encourages a free-flowing and spontaneous list of ideas with few limiting constraints. After the list is assembled, it can be whittled down to a shortlist of the most promising ideas.

- **Free association**

  Sigmund Freud made it famous, making the unconscious conscious. But free association can work for more than patients with psychological problems. Let your mind go when dreaming up new concoctions in the kitchen. Have a family member make a random list of various words or a targeted list of culinary words and see what pops into your head.

- **Opposite attractions**

  Sometimes it works for marriages, so why not see if some opposite attractions work for your culinary creations? When it comes to flavors, explore pairing sour and sweet, like mangoes and salsa or balsamic vinegar and raspberries. Salty and sweet

are a well-known match made in heaven. Keep a notepad next to your bed in case an idea suddenly appears; the moments just before and immediately after you sleep can be very creative times for some people.

- **Discordant events**

  Disagreement and conflict can breed new ideas, even if they're odd, like the invisible dog or a "pet rock." Why did it take so long to put wheels on luggage so we wouldn't have to drag our suitcases through the airport? One of the tastiest ideas in recent times is turning a flower bouquet into a cookie bouquet. When can something that clashes become something brilliantly creative?

- **Drawing a map for success**

  What would it look like if you made a picture of your dream business? Sometimes pictures are worth a thousand words. Some of us think visually. Try sketching a map or visual representation of your route to success, tracing the ingredients from the garden or a local supplier to your end product. Or use one of the many online apps or a free website, like Freemind, to guide your efforts.

or contents, there's plenty of evidence that a catchy name grabs the attention of a potential customer passing by. In that fraction of a second, you'll either have a sale, or not.

Take chocolate biscotti. Perhaps it's crunchy, made with fair-trade certified cacao powder and almonds and can be enjoyed as a snack with coffee or tea. Why not call it Double-Down Chocolate Almond Crunch? Adding a little alliteration, plus including another defining ingredient (almonds), may trigger a pang of hunger — and spur an impulse purchase.

Avoid obsessing over naming your product, but have fun with it. Keep your market, positioning and other marketing considerations in mind, since your name should echo the other aspects of your marketing. If you are planning a product line, consider a name that can be easily carried across the entire line in some way.

Before you settle on a name, however, try running it by the Internet to make sure you're not violating any existing trademarks. "Cease and desist"

A Company Name

Besides coming up with memorable, descriptive, relevant or provocative names for your products, you'll also need to decide on the legal name for your company itself. Many CFOs have a fictional business name used with the public that's distinctive, easy to say and spell, memorable and that captures the essence of what you sell or evokes feelings you want associated with your business. This fictional name is referred to as a DBA, "doing business as." There's nothing wrong with using your own name in the business name, or a variation of it, like Bonnie's Baked Goods (with alliteration) or Aunt Emma's Pride. You may have a more personalized name for your business, too, if you operate as an LLC or corporation (covered in Chapter 11), plus a DBA. Your business name is part of your marketing, so take the time to choose it carefully.

Before you proceed, run the name by friends and family for feedback. Check to see if the domain name is still available in case you want to create a website. If you think there's a possibility you might scale up later on, check to see if you can trademark the name with the US Patent and Trademark Office (USPTO). The website domain name can be checked for free on whois.net; to complete a free USPTO search using the "trademark electronic search system," type your name into their search engine on uspto.gov. Even if you do not want to trademark your name, you will still need to register it in your state through your secretary of state or other licensing department; your state will have some form of free search feature to see if the name you want can be used there.

notes from an attorney representing a company with a product by the same name as yours can sour an otherwise exciting product launch. Here's one of the items that came up on our search for our hypothetical Double-Down Chocolate Almond Crunch: Creamy Almond Crunch SQUARES™, trademarked by Ghirardelli, a multinational. Given this, we'd feel okay to proceed with our product name. If we wanted to take this product national and scale up, we'd complete a trademark search with the US Patent and Trademark Office (see Company Name sidebar) to be a 100 percent certain, while protecting our name from infringement by another company.

Labeling

Great news. The cottage food law for your state dictates exactly what must be on the label. If you're not selling wholesale, you won't need those UPC symbols or the product nutritional information panel you see on packaged goods. In fact, besides a list of ingredients in order of greatest to least use by weight, most states only require a sentence with your name and contact information, plus a sentence that says something like "Manufactured in a home kitchen" or "Not prepared in a state-approved commercial food facility," the exact wording usually specified by your state. While not required for labels under most cottage food laws, weight, units or volume measurement, can be added; note, however, that weight is always net, referring only to the contents and not the packaging.

Only food companies with "annual gross sales made or business done in sales to consumers that is not more than $500,000 or have annual gross sales made or business done in sales of food to consumers of not more than $50,000 are exempt" from nutritional labeling

Pucker Ups label from Inn Serendipity Bed & Breakfast.

John D. Ivanko / innserendipity.com

Pucker Ups

Dill Pickles

Peacefully pickled by Lisa Kivirist, Inn Serendipity, W7843 County Road P, Browntown, WI 53522
Date of canning: July 14, 2014

Ingredients: Organic cucumbers, water, vinegar, sugar, pickling spice, organic dill weed, organic garlic, mustard seed.

This product was made in a private home not subject to state licensing or inspection.

Refrigerate after opening.
Shelf life: 12 months   Price: $10

requirements, according to the FDA; for lots more detail, see their website: fda.gov.

While not explicitly required by state cottage food laws, it's advisable to take extra precautions by labeling your product and identifying any allergens, such as milk, eggs, tree nuts, soy, peanuts and wheat. For example, if they have allergens in their kitchen, many CFOs elect to add a sentence like "Made in a facility that processes peanuts, soy and wheat." For most operators working from a home kitchen, this would be the case.

Be careful on any health claims you make on your label or in any marketing materials. If you say that your product reduces the risk of a disease or medical condition, this claim must be approved by the United States' FDA, a process both highly involved and complicated. If you claim that an ingredient in your product improves a function, such as "calcium builds strong bones," you will need to compile legitimate research from reputable and neutral sources. If you make a nutrient content claim, such as your muffins are high in fiber, low in fat or low-glycemic, the package must have a full nutritional label that may be more complicated and costly than you may want to go. You cannot file for an exemption when you make a health claim.

Beyond the state cottage food requirements, the rest of the label design is up to you and your fancy. Thanks to color printers and various self-adhesive label options for home printing, if you have some mastery of a computer, take great photographs, have talent as an illustrator or can type, you can pull off a homespun label in very small quantities to stick to your jars, boxes, containers or tins, whatever their size.

If you have enough volume, however, there are several options for printing professional-looking labels on par with anything you'd find at a supermarket or specialty food store. Thanks to breakthroughs in

UPC Codes for Wholesale Customers

A Universal Product Code, or UPC, is a series of bars and 12-digit numbers unique to each packaged item you may sell, issued by the GS1 US Partner Connections Program (gs1us.org). Though they are not required by law, UPCs are usually a necessity if you offer your products wholesale to retailers and distributors, as they allow these customers to store, stock and track sales of your items. These codes can also be secured and printed by companies like ABB Labels (abblabels.com) or Simply Barcodes (upccode.net). Each UPC code includes both a manufacturer identification number and a unique item code. Note that UPCs are different from Stock Keeping Units or SKUs, covered in Chapter 14.

digital printing, Lightning Labels (lightninglabels.com), Wizard Labels (wizardlabels.com), PrintRunner (printrunner.com) and YourLabelsNow (yourlabelsnow.com) are four companies you might consider that can quickly produce smaller print runs at reasonable prices.

Logo: Picturing Your Product, Company or Brand

Whether it's a symbol, a graphic, a word or a creative combination of two or three of the above, a logo helps define your company and its products and makes what you create more memorable to your customers. A logo can be as simple as Nike's swoosh or as intricate as Harvard University's shield with its Latin motto, *Veritas*. While you don't need one to operate a business successfully, a logo can help, especially as you expand. A well-designed logo lends credibility and an aura of professionalism, and may help reinforce your price strategy if it's on the higher side compared to your competition.

When designing your logo, consider how and where you might be using it. Will you be paying to reproduce it in four colors on a label, or photocopying it in black and white at the top of your solicitation letterhead? Maybe you'll be doing both color and black and white. Detailed logos can rarely be reduced to small sizes on product labels and still be legible.

For basic, low-cost logo options, review various online logo makers such as LogoGenie (logogenie.net) or Graphic Springs (graphicsprings.com). These websites walk you through the logo design process for free online. If you like what you created, you can download the final art for less than ten dollars.

Slogan

> "The Freshest in the Business"
> "Bottling up Nature"
> "Quality. Taste. Baked right, every time."

Similar to a logo, but written as text, a slogan captures in a phrase what your business is about in a memorable, catchy and creative way, with the intent of helping close a sale. If you distilled your product to its essence, what words would you use to describe it?

Also like a logo, a slogan, while not required, can help position your products in the minds of your customers and reinforce the personality of

the brand you're creating. If you say "fair and balanced" enough, people believe it (even if it isn't necessarily true). Can you complete these sentences?

"When E.F. Hutton talks, people _____."
"_____ of Champions."

If you can't fill in the blanks of both slogans, it means either you weren't alive when they were used or you weren't in the target market for these products.

Slogans can be used on your letterhead, website, beneath your company name or tied to your logo in some way. Unlike your business name and logo, however, slogans can, and often do, change over the years. In 1979, Toyota proclaimed: "Oh, what a feeling!" Now, it's "Moving forward." So if you discover a more compelling slogan, perhaps something a customer says, change it.

Safely Packaging a Powerful Punch Line

With your name, label and logo in hand, the next step is getting your item packaged in a way that ensures its quality, safety and compelling presentation. One thing is certain — as much as possible, your packaging should allow the customer to see your product. People eat with their eyes first.

When working at a large ad agency in Chicago years ago, we became familiar with the expression, "selling the sizzle, not the steak." In some cases, the actual product attributes themselves were tangential to the messaging and claims made about the product. We were creating a personality or image around an item, a national brand, and having that personality carry over to the product itself, so people would be persuaded to buy it next time they needed a box of cereal for breakfast. What does a cartoon character have to do with a nourishing way to start your day with a cereal breakfast? The answer is, it doesn't really matter, so long as the customer feels the emotions and connects them with a certain product so that as a result they select one brand over another. Finish the sentence: "They're _____!"

By their very nature, many specialty food products and cottage food items are impulse, on-the-spot purchases. You could be selling muffins at a community event where hungry kids tug at a mother's sleeve or setting out stacks of your granola bars at a Little League game. Besides being able to see what your product looks like, having a professional and engaging package and label can be the difference between landing a sale or missing one.

Whether or not your state law specifically requires product packaging, safely wrap your item for two compelling reasons:

(a) sturdy packaging prevents food contamination and ensures safe transport;
(b) unique packaging can be a marketing advantage.

The first and most important issue is food safety. Wrapping your product makes sure it will not be exposed to the elements, either on your end as you transport it to your sales venue or customer or when your customer brings it home or delivers it to the final destination.

Your style or design of packaging depends on what you're selling, but it's especially relevant to baked goods, candy and anything what won't already be in a jar, like jam. For basic baked goods, food-grade plastic bags work well. As you start out, these could just be ziplock bags from the grocery store. As you sell more product, check out a bakery packaging supply outlet to order bulk bags or various-sized cardboard pastry boxes. These boxes can be important if you make something fragile that requires extra transport protection, such as decorated cupcakes. Sources of cardboard boxes for baked goods include KitchenKrafts (kitchenkrafts.com), MrTakeOutBags.com (mrtakeoutbags.com) and BRP Box Shop (brpboxshop.com).

Thoughtful, colorful packaging draws customers in and can showcase your product. For baked and other goods, the range of packaging options can be overwhelming. There's clear plastic sleeves, paper bags, display boxes, decorative tins and for the eco-minded, corn- or soy-based natural, biodegradable alternatives. Each has a cost that needs to be considered when fixing the price for your product, a subject covered in the next chapter.

If you're selling baked goods directly, perhaps by delivering them to an office, large boxes might be a good choice. You might even explore reuseable delivery boxes, with a deposit that comes in the form of a discount off a future order. If you're selling a fancy edible cookie bouquet for the

holidays or anniversaries, then a food-grade basket and plastic wrap might make the most sense.

Some packaging costs more. You'll have to decide if it's worth it to elicit an impulse buy or increase sales. You can buy cupcake boxes that hold two cupcakes in an insert and come with a carrying handle and a "window," a plastic section on one side so you can see inside the box. These can cost up to one dollar each, but may make your customer feel like they have received a beautifully wrapped present. If you're selling at a market or event and someone is carrying around that cute box, they may serve as a free walking advertisement for your product. Adding a piece of colorful tissue paper in a bakery box may add a frilly gift appeal.

Because standard boxes for baked goods come blank, don't forget to add a sticker label or stamp that displays your business name and contact info prominently, so customers can reorder or have a quick reference for referrals. There's no need to add the extra expense of printing on cardboard boxes. Feel free to dress up the box even further with a ribbon or other colored stickers or stamps. These simple touches add inexpensive glitz to your product and announce that they hold something truly special inside.

Adding an extra bling to packaging, like a metallic ribbon, can increase the perceived value of your product and command a higher price.

For canned items, glass jars work perfectly; they are, by default of health and safety issues addressed by hot water bath processing, the only way such goods can be sold. But you can still add a little frugal extra to dress these jars up and boost your item's perceived value. A cloth ribbon around a canning jar adds that "gift" appeal. Place a small round of cloth material under the canning jar ring for a pop of color; a paper cupcake liner may also work well under the canning jar ring.

"The whole presentation, the pink box, the ribbons, the way it was put together was really, really cool. Everyone loved it."

— Harmonie Kuhl, Corona, California, a customer raving about Cookies Your Way

Inn Serendipity's creative packaging on display. John D. Ivanko

One clever way to cover the requirements related to labeling your jars is to use the top and bottom of the jars for the product name, ingredient list and other required verbiage. In this way, your customers can see your wonderfully preserved relish or pickles.

For specialty food products that are sold wholesale, packaging is particularly important. The container for the product should be comparable in size, both by weight and dimensions, to your competition. Make sure your case size is the standard twelve units. Remember, you want to make it easy for retailers to stock your items on their shelves.

The look of your product — its name, label, logo and packaging — is just the start. In the following marketing chapters, we'll explore some of the other aspects of building a brand and growing a customer base eager to purchase your products and support you and your business.

Bottom of the jar label, with required information presented per the cottage food law in your state, like the date, name of person doing the production and the "private home" disclaimer line. John D. Ivanko

Top of the jar labels from Equinox Community Farm, with key information presented, including company and product name. John D. Ivanko

5

Getting the Price Right

B Y NOW, YOU REALIZE THAT THERE'S A LOT MORE to a food product than the product itself. Sure, it has to taste great, but plenty of other factors determine whether customers will try your product and keep coming back for more. Pricing your product right can be a big part of the equation. It can be the difference, too, between actually making money and just having a hobby.

Business Expenses

Before getting into the nitty-gritty of pricing your product, you'll need to get some sense of what it may take to get your business off the ground from a financial perspective. Below is a breakdown of the three general types of business expenses we'll cover in greater detail in the Business Management section:

- Start-up expenses: including local, state and federal licenses, registration fees, and utensils, pots or pans and kitchen equipment.
- Fixed expenses: while very limited, these could include a business telephone line, hosting cost for your website and domain name registration.
- Variable expenses: including ingredients, packaging, gas for delivery and rental fees for a booth or exhibitor table.

Unlike a food product company that produces their items in a commercial kitchen, licensed home kitchen or rented space in a licensed facility, your state's cottage food law means you don't have this expensive start-up or fixed overhead expense. However, because of your setup, you cannot deduct your utility costs (electricity or natural gas) or the use of your home kitchen as business expenses.

Self-worth: Valuing Your Time

It's perhaps one of the more vexing issues of our day: How much is time worth? While the never-ending debate rages on about the minimum wage and exorbitant CEO salaries, when it comes to considering the labor involved in producing your products, can you get away with charging enough for your products to pay yourself, too? Price your products too high and you may only sell a few; price them too low and you may not earn enough to reimburse yourself for the ingredients or cover your labor. Economists call this "elasticity of demand": the relationship between price and quantity demanded of a product by customers. Your market feasibility study, covered in Chapter 9, will help you determine your product's fair market value.

You may feel your hard work and skills are worth fifty dollars per hour when decorating a four-tier wedding cake that takes about twelve hours to make and deliver. But what if where you live the going rate for a wedding cake like this is only $350? This is far below your labor costs and other variable costs, including the high-quality ingredients you decided to use. If they're just starting out, some CFOs may proceed anyway, looking to grow customers by referrals, grow volume and then, down the line, when they have a great reputation, raise prices to better reflect the costs and labor involved.

As explored previously, some of us define success beyond the merely financial. Maybe it's about time for delicious, local and organic sourdough breads to be available where you live, but due to the realities of the economy, your customers are only willing to pay $2.50 per loaf. In cases like this, the joy of running your own business, making social connections and a host of other considerations can compensate you in ways cold hard cash may never. Plus, when the economy picks up, you can raise your prices with it; economists call this "relationship inflation". In many cases, you may be forced to raise your prices because the costs of your ingredients are likewise increasing.

Pricing Your Product

Now that you have an idea as to some of your business expenses and the tricky part of determining the value of your labor, you can start to think about how to price your product. Unfortunately, there's no steadfast rule, guideline or principle for this.

There are, however, several ways to determine the end retail price for a food item sold directly to the public:

1. Parity Pricing

By far the easiest way to set the price for your product is to just sell it for a little more or a little less than a similar product already sold in your community. If the going rate for a dozen muffins from an area bakery is $17, then your price could be about the same if you adopt this approach. Once your customers taste the difference, most will choose your better-tasting muffins, prices being roughly the same.

This approach may hit a snag if you decide that your competition is the bakery department of a local supermarket, selling that same dozen muffins on special for $12 per dozen. It's unlikely they use the same quality ingredients and probably don't make them from scratch like you do. At this point, your product positioning, packaging and other marketing come into play, to differentiate your product and justify the higher price you'll need to charge for it.

A mini chalk board sign provides an easy and attractive way to clearly communicate the price for your products.
JOHN D. IVANKO

2. Cost-input Calculation

A far more accurate way to set your item price would be to review your food costs by ingredient, add them together, then multiply by three to six times to cover your labor, packaging, overhead like electric or gas use, and delivery. The higher multiplier would account for the quality of your ingredients and other personal variables, such as more difficult recipes to prepare or the venue you sell at charging a fee. To simplify this calculation, some CFOs just use the most expensive ingredients as a benchmark and go from there to calculate a fair retail price.

Because this approach to pricing your product is much more involved, a cost-input calculator is available via our book's website (homemadeforsale.com).

3. Market Value

While related to parity pricing, market-value pricing carefully considers where you're selling your product. As we'll see in the next chapter, the distribution of your items may dictate what you're able to charge for them. Selling muffins at a weekly farmers' market where other vendors are competing with baked goods and edibles may be very different from selling them at a holiday bazaar where you have the only baked-goods display and everyone is in a festive, shopping mood; the holiday bazaar should naturally lend itself to higher prices.

The more high-end or upscale the event or place, the more you can charge, because in most cases, your customers will not be as price sensitive as people browsing the aisles for a deal or special. Don't underestimate the pricing power of attractive packaging. Dressing up your box with some ribbons and colorful fabric can reinforce your premium price.

Like buying stock in a company or investing in real estate, the price is determined by what someone is willing to pay. Your customer is always queen or king. If your product is priced too high, what you sell doesn't match your target market's aspirations or your packaging doesn't reflect your positioning well enough, you may find yourself returning home with what you made. Decisions about ingredients, packaging and labeling play a direct role in determining the profitability of your product.

Never fear. Your market research and feasibility study will help you to better determine realistic pricing for your products. Don't feel you should, or even have to, compete on price. In most cases, your products will be far superior to most of the competition already in the market where you live, because yours are homemade, fresh or custom ordered. Whatever you do, don't pay people to buy your product because you are selling it for less than it is worth.

On the flip side, your products may be the only premium-priced items in the market, allowing you to command the top dollar from those customers eager to get their hands on something available nowhere else. Interestingly, there are people who, for various reasons, will only buy the most expensive item on a restaurant menu or at the jewelry store or winery. Justified or not, they equate quality with price. In marketing jargon, it's called a "premium pricing strategy", also called "skimming," as in taking the cream

Custom Cookie Favors at a Premium

If the artist Vincent van Gogh came back in contemporary cottage food times and baked, he undoubtedly would be Jennifer Evans. A self-taught cookie artist, Evans blends sugar cookie shapes with vivid frosting colors and design techniques to create decorative cookies that look so much like mini works of art that you almost consider not eating them. Until you do. And then, as her loyal customers attest, you'll just order another batch. From personalized pink pajama-shaped cookies for preteen girl sleepovers to multiple variations on Valentine's Day hearts, Cookies Plz provides Evans with a rainbow-inspired palette of creative outlets and income opportunities.

Evans' underlying success in starting Cookies Plz lies in her ability to connect the dots when it comes to business opportunity. By creating a niche business that targets those wanting — and willing to pay a premium for — unique, vibrantly colored cookies customized perfectly for their special occasion, Evans takes full advantage of her cottage food law to make money and have fun operating from the comfort of her family-centered home.

"No other job beats making cookies at night in my kitchen in my pajamas with a glass of wine," shares Evans in her warm Texas drawl. When a neighbor brought over decorated sugar cookies and shared her recipe, Evans saw an opportunity. "That neighbor's cookie delivery happened in February 2011, and our cottage food law in Texas took effect in September. It gave me a few months to practice." Her motivation to start the business came from wanting to showcase her cookie-making talents while making a little money on the side. Evans focuses on creating thick and sturdy cookies in custom shapes and themes and topped with colorful royal icing that dries solid and smooth.

"My first cookies were outright ugly, but friends and family encouraged me to keep at it," admits Evans. She found a supportive and helpful "cookie community" both online and in her local community of other Texas home bakers. Evans found a great resource in "The Sweet Adventures of Sugarbelle" blog (sweetsugarbelle.com), including a sample cookie pricing chart that serves as an industry standard in the home-baked sugar cookie market. "If someone wants to order my cookies and they live too far for me

Name: Jennifer Evans

Business: Cookies Plz (Fort Worth, TX)

Website: facebook.com/CookiesPlz

Products: decorated sugar cookies

Sales Venue: direct delivery of special orders via telephone, text and e-mail; custom orders

Annual Sales: $5,100

Jennifer Evans decorating her star cookies using a piping bag.
Courtesy of Cookies Plz

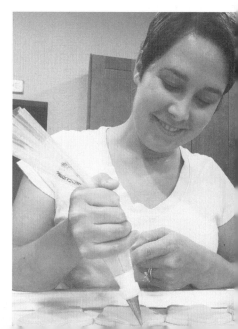

to deliver, I refer them to someone I know closer to them. These bakers do the same for me. Cookie bakers are super-collaborative."

"It's important to know your strengths and weaknesses. I am definitely not an artist," Evans says. Looking at her cookies, though, you'd beg to differ.

Turns out you don't need to be an artist to lend an artistic touch to craft cookies. Say hello to Kopykake (kopykake.com), a nifty specialized projector that projects any image downward so it can be easily traced onto cakes and cookies or any other material. The light (and thereby heat) is on the top so the tracing process won't melt the icing. "I spent over three hundred dollars on my Kopykake, a big purchase for me, but I saw it as an investment. I can justify buying professional-grade items because I'm running a business and not just a kitchen hobby."

The core customers for Cookies Plz come from upscale families with disposable income looking to buy one-of-a-kind, personalized favors for a party or an event. Her cookies garner an amazing reaction due to their unique designs accompanied by eye-catching colors. "Competitive soccer moms make up my most loyal customers. They love ordering cookies in their kid's team colors and personalized with each child's name and number," adds Evans. "Rather than pay three dollars for a plastic party favor or some candy, folks like to order customized cookies made just for their event." Baby showers, themed birthday parties and weddings serve as potential markets for cookie favors.

Her on-the-go soccer moms often send orders by text from their smartphones. Evans confirms details via text, then sends a PayPal "request for payment" a week before pickup.

"My minimum order is three dozen cookies. I've learned it just isn't worth my time to take out my mixer and supplies for anything less than that," shares Evans. Her prices range from $1.75 for a small, basic cookie, which would be her simple shapes like basketballs, baseballs or diplomas with a maximum of three colors in addition to black and white. Personalization or monograms cost an extra 25 cents per cookie. She charges up to seven dollars for an extra-large, elaborately decorated version which involves lots of colors and details that require multiple drying steps or labor-intensive techniques like brush embroidery or quilting.

"Another equipment investment I made is a heat sealer. It allows me to seal a plastic bag around my cookie," says Evans. "People buying cookies as

favors like this. With the sealed plastic wrap, these cookies look like they came from a large, professional bakery. Plus the wrap increases shelf life by keeping my cookies fresher longer, so I don't have to make them all the day before." The heat-seal bag also helps protect the cookies when customers transport them home.

Time management is a priority for Evans. Her family and young kids remain the top priority. "I require folks to pick up their orders, which saves me a lot of time driving and delivering. Plus the moms who buy my cookies are often out and about anyway so another stop doesn't phase them," explains Evans. She aims to limit herself to one cookie order a week to keep her family time in check. She homeschools her daughters and makes the cookies after the kids go to bed. "I turned down three Valentine's Day orders in February, but I've learned it's better to do that and keep things manageable and fun."

Set up as a sole proprietorship, Cookies Plz generated more than $5,100 in sales last year, with approximately $4,500 in expenses. "I made equipment investments last year. My biggest challenge with managing my expenses is deciding where to invest my money. Do I want to be able to further my business by attending expensive classes and buying equipment or do I use the money for what I really started my business for, which is supplementing our income? Plus ingredients keep increasing in cost. But I'm learning to manage things better as I go and keep evaluating my pricing to make sure payments reflect my inputs," sums up Evans.

"With cookies like these, I've realized folks are willing to pay a premium for something awesome and different. That's where I deliver."

off the top of a jar of milk. If you can back up such an approach with your great-tasting product, why not? It's worked well for Apple, Tiffany and Tesla for their respective products.

Variable Savings

While we touched on the value of your labor and some of your fixed start-up costs, where you can cut corners without impacting the quality of your product may be with your packaging and the ingredients themselves.

Slashing Ingredient Costs

There's nothing like sourcing some of your ingredients from your own gardens or growing fields. From pumpkin for muffins, raspberries for preserves and cucumbers for pickles, using your own ingredients (if your state's law allows it) can cut your variable costs considerably.

If that's not feasible, bulk up. Don't overlook ways to buy bulk ingredients at prices just over wholesale through a food cooperative or buying club. Food cooperatives are member-owned grocery stores that specialize in more health-conscious food options. Membership fees are nominal and give you access to discounted pricing and better sourcing options with a focus on local and sustainable agricultural products and specialty foods. Food co-ops often have bulk aisles; they can special-order a fifty-pound bag of flour or sugar for you, often at an additional discount.

If you don't have a food cooperative where you live, check and see if there might be a buying club that offers similar options. A buying club allows a group of people to collectively place an order with a distributor. Because of the volume, the distributor can offer wholesale pricing. Other options include United Natural Foods (unfi.com), a food wholesaler, or a food distributor that specifically serves food businesses in your community.

Don't rule out supermarkets. Some chains, like Whole Foods Market, offer a bulk aisle and may be able to order a full bulk bag for you. Warehouse clubs may also be an option for large case-size packs of key ingredients; increasingly some warehouse clubs, such as Costco, sell large bulk bags and even organic items.

Another way to cut down on your ingredient costs is by purchasing "seconds" or overstocks directly from area farmers. You don't need perfect tomatoes to make salsa; a box with a few blemishes you can cut around will

Securing a bushel of pear "seconds" from a local farm can be a great way to cut variable food costs. JOHN D. IVANKO

work fine. This works great if you're into producing preserves, marmalades, salsas or pickles. Some of these farms might end up partnering with you by helping you sell your value-added products to their customers (if allowed by your cottage food law).

Penny Pinching on Packaging and Kitchen Supplies

The cost for various packing materials can add up, reducing your profit per item. So why not try to locate some of the materials you might need that may cost you little to nothing? The following short list offers several ways to locate packaging, kitchen supplies and other items at prices much less than full retail.

Craigslist: craigslist.org

This classified online portal can reveal a wide assortment of items relatively close to home at bargain basement prices. It does require a time commitment to check the postings, but if you decide you need a stainless steel counter, you may find one for sale in town.

Freecycle: freecycle.org

A penny saved is a penny earned. Look to your community for items you might need for your business, without paying a cent for them. This online portal for your city or region allows you to post items you either need or want to get rid of. No money changes hands; everything is free. We load up on our canning jars this way.

Ebay: ebay.com

It's the most popular online auction site in North America. If it has ever been produced, it's probably listed here, sometimes at a price so cheap you wonder why someone would even go through the effort of listing it. If you're lucky, you might find odd lots of boxes, baskets and a dizzying array of items you can use in your packaging or kitchen.

Etsy: etsy.com

An e-commerce website featuring handmade craft items and supplies. It can also be a place for packaging design ideas or, if your cottage food law allows it, online mail-order sales.

Co-author Lisa Kivirist with one of her fresh strawberries harvested from her organic growing fields. Always remember to eat the strawberry. John D. Ivanko

Thrift stores

Don't underestimate your local thrift store for attractive baskets, containers, boxes, ribbon or other packaging materials for pennies on the dollar.

Your pricing may also need to account for any promotional costs and food samples given away at events. But as we cover in the next chapter, most cottage food enterprises will launch without the need to spend much on promotion.

6

Moving Your Product to Market

GROWING YOUR CUSTOMER BASE is essential for growing sales. While people may love your product, they can only eat so much of it. If you want to maintain or increase your sales, you'll need to attract new customers through referrals, seek out new sales venues or explore other marketing approaches related to this P of marketing: the Place where you're selling your items, covered in this chapter.

Just as it defines your product, the cottage food law in your state will specify the venue or venues at which you can sell your products. The greater the flexibility in sales channels permitted by your state, the better the opportunities for distribution, allowing you to reach a wider market. If you're forced into only one sales venue or outlet, then you'll have to see how many different outlets you can sell at to achieve your sales goals. For example, several states are so restrictive that cottage food operators can only sell at farmers' markets; in fact, in several cases, the cottage food law only applies to farmers! But this is the exception; the vast majority of states permit sales in so many venues that you'll need to decide which ones work best for you.

Sales Venues: Places to Sell

Most states provide several potential venues where you can sell your goods to the public. Very few, however, permit mail order. Because of how the cottage food laws are written and with rare exception, no sales of your products can be made in a state other than the one you reside in. At the time of printing, only fourteen states permit selling wholesale, a process by which another retailer sells your product to a customer for you. While most states require you to sell directly to the customer, there are quite a variety of ways to do so, each covered next.

Since gasoline or diesel fuel isn't getting any cheaper, evaluate just how far you need to go to deliver your product to your customers. Besides fuel costs and possible tolls or parking meters, consider how much time you want to be stuck in traffic or running around the city dropping off orders. Are you in the delivery business or the bakery business?

Evaluate your set of wheels as well. Do you have the right kind of vehicle to transport cases of jams and jellies or a large and fragile wedding cake? If you're using your vehicle more, it's reasonable to anticipate that there will be additional repair and maintenance costs. If your markets are nearby and your orders are small, see if delivery may be made by bicycle or on foot.

Direct Customer Deliveries

For many CFOs, distributing your product is the easiest part of your business, if your family members can't wait to place advance orders, your office co-workers just need an order form or your church has already welcomed you to set up a display in the lobby of the community room after Sunday service to distribute advance orders. Many CFOs prefer direct sales since they like the certainty of the advance order, especially if it comes with a prepayment or deposit.

Selling to family, friends or office workers may be awkward at first, or make you uncomfortable. It's not unlike teens reaching out to neighbors during school or organizational fundraising campaigns. How did this disconnect happen? Somewhere along the line as our local economy evolved into a global marketplace, we lost the personal connection between products and the people who make them. Today, most foods are made by anonymous people (or machines in factories) located thousands of miles away. As a result, selling to friends can feel odd.

But why wouldn't your best friend buy your granola bars instead of some national brand — especially if yours are priced fairly and taste great? Chances are your muffins, cookies or pickles are far superior to those shelf-stable national brands, because you don't pack them full of preservatives, chemicals, fillers or other mystery ingredients. Your heart went into making them.

If you find yourself suddenly grappling with the fact that you're charging for what you once gave away free, think about coming up with new products your friends have never tried. Or emphasize how your friends are linked to the marketing story: they're helping support your dream, your business and a shared local economy. In the end, people are more likely to buy things from people they trust, admire, respect and care about. Of course, you can always donate some of your products to a fundraiser or silent auction when your friends give you a call.

Home Pickup

Certain states allow cottage food products to be picked up at your home. You could even offer a discount off a future order to those customers who do so, since having them pick up their order saves you both time and money for fuel. You'll need to evaluate, however, if this is a route you want to take. People get busy, miss appointments or come at the wrong time. You'll also need to check with your city and zoning department to see if any restrictions on the books apply to you.

Sampling out HeathGlen's Farm & Kitchen products at a community event.
COURTESY OF HEATHGLEN'S FARM & KITCHEN

Community Events

One of the more popular ways to distribute your products directly to your customers is by going to where your customers are. Holiday festivals, shopping bazaars, arts and craft fairs, farmers' markets, community markets, walk-a-thons and community-wide tourism-related events may welcome cottage food vendors.

While there is usually a fee associated with a booth space at these events, the cost may be worth it if the event draws a large crowd and has strong marketing support — the organizers may even promote your enterprise as a vendor on their website, in printed materials, via social media or all of the above.

One of the easiest ways to pick up new customers is one bite at a time through samples, assuming the community event organizers or venue allow it. Because your products are non-hazardous, you'll have an advantage over

other commercial vendors who may have products requiring refrigeration. That doesn't guarantee, however, that a health inspector passing through the event will like how you're sampling out the items on toothpicks or spoons. The event may also have a policy restricting what you can sample and how — or require, if you sample items, additional liability insurance beyond which you feel you want to commit.

Even if an event draws in a crowd, there's no guarantee you'll blow out of your products. There is an uncertainty that comes with selling at an event: inclement weather reducing attendance; guessing how much of which product you should bring; a competing vendor with a cheaper product in a booth across from yours. One barometer you can use to gage the potential market for your products at a particular event is the number of vendors already selling there and the number of years they have been doing so. Another consideration is the appropriateness of your product to the event itself. For example, pickles and chutneys may be a hit at a farmers' market while dried soup mixes or decorated cookies may draw greater interest at a gift-focused holiday bazaar.

Holiday Bazaar or Farmers' Market Packing List

If you think a packing list for attending and selling an event is overkill, don't. The difference between a fun, organized, successful and profitable event and one that's not can be as simple as a forgotten money belt (or change drawer), an attractive tablecloth or a chair to sit on when there's a lull in the crowds.

[ ] Table

[ ] Chair

[ ] Tablecloth

[ ] Display gear: cake stands, baskets, risers, etc.

[ ] Pricing cards for each item; people want to see what something costs (without having to ask you)

[ ] Money belt or change drawer, with plenty of small change and the ability to break large bills without a crisis

[ ] Credit card processing forms and device, if you accept them

[ ] Attractive table signage with your business name and other particulars

[ ] Business cards or order forms for your products

[ ] Masking or duct tape

[ ] Permanent marker

[ ] Bags for customers

Selling at Market: Tips to Return Home "Sold Out"

Over a dozen states' cottage food laws limit sales to public events like farmers' markets, fairs or other community gatherings. While restrictive, you need to figure out how to thrive within the system you have in your state. (Of course, you can also advocate for expanded legislation.)

Rather than seeing your sales venue potential as half empty, view it as half full, adjusting your strategy to sell at the best public market outlets you can find. Some ideas to boost your market or event bottom line include the following:

- **Cross-promote**
  What do you sell that pairs perfectly with something else at the market? Do you make relish and someone else sells sausages? Do you sell pound cake and another farmer sells fresh strawberries or blueberries that would make the perfect complement? Connect with these vendors and explore your cross-selling opportunities.

- **Cater to kids**
  You always see kids at markets. Often they look a little bit bored while their parents or caregivers negotiate more time to linger and shop. Provide a solution: small treats for the kids, something to occupy them and satisfy their hunger. Selling something easy to hold and eat in a kid-appealing shape could score some points, like a cake pop or pickle on a stick.

- **Offer multiples**
  Everyone loves a special deal. Look at how some of the farmers promote their produce. Borrow a couple tactics, like "buy one, get one free" or volume discount pricing: "3 for $10."

- **Seek shade**
  If possible, visit the market beforehand and see how the sun hits it. Try to confirm a booth space in as much shade as possible to help preserve your products, especially if you have baked goods or candies.

- **Barter**
  At the end of the market, especially if you have extra fresh fare like loaves of bread, barter with other vendors for some take-home treats. Common after the market has closed, these barter scenes provide an extra bonus: building community and cultivating relationships.

The display of HeathGlen's Farm & Kitchen products feature signage that conveys how their products can be paired with cheese, meat and wine. Courtesy of HeathGlen's Farm & Kitchen

Sponsoring a community bake-off, can-off or cook-off may be a quick way to reach potential customers, sample out some of your products to participants or spectators and establish credibility, brand or company awareness and interest in your products. You may even be able to be one of the judges on the panel. This may require a financial investment or, if you approach it right, an in-kind (i.e., non-cash) donation of products that will be given away to winning participants or volunteers helping out.

As the cottage food movement continues to grow, opportunity abounds to collectively join forces for cross-pollination and cooperative marketing. At the forefront of this effort, cottage food entrepreneurs in California launched the Bay Area Homemade Market (bayareahomemademarket. com), a festive fair specifically designed for CFOs to co-market and attract potential customers interested in sampling and purchasing their unique products. These events — with a tag line of "connecting the community one bite at a time" — showcase the potential of cottage food businesses working together to champion each other and create situations where everyone has an improved opportunity to sell their products.

Special Events or Weddings

One of the more lucrative and labor-intensive outlets for your products might be weddings or special community or corporate events. Being careful not to cross the legal line of being a caterer instead of a cottage food entrepreneur, baking enough muffins for a company's annual breakfast meeting or a wedding cake to feed a hundred can translate to big bucks.

Such events require extra planning: a contract, invoicing and even liability insurance might be necessary before you take this type of order. Given the size and dollar amount of the order, getting everything in writing is a must, for both parties' sake. Accepting a nominal advance deposit would be expected if you are to hold a date; requiring full payment a month before the wedding date would also not be out of line. We've included a sample contract for reference on this book's website; see homemadeforsale.com.

Wholesale

More than a dozen states allow various forms of wholesale or indirect sales. This allows you to sell to a venue like a retailer or restaurant that then resells your product. For these transactions to take place, you will

Queen of Cake Creates Wedding Cakes Fit for Royalty

"Boutique style." "Couture." "Knowledge of the latest trends." No, we're not talking about high-end fashion off the Paris runway. This is how the Queen of Cake and Events describes her creations, thanks to the creative vision of the "queen" herself, Suzy Zimmermann.

"In Texas we like things big with glitz and glamour, so of course you're going to want to bring that attitude to the cake for the biggest day of your life," chuckles Zimmermann. But this is not glitz with no substance underneath. A trained and accomplished cake artist, Zimmermann exemplifies how to create a professional, high-end business out of the comfort of one's own kitchen.

"I originally learned how to bake and decorate cakes from my grandmother when I was still a child, and I've been hooked ever since," explains Zimmermann. She originally started Queen of Cake in 2005, renting commercial kitchen space until the Texas Cottage Food Law passed in 2011. "Working from my home kitchen really helped me grow my business as I could bake and decorate much more efficiently and save on rental costs."

While her cakes shout custom design and fancy details, Zimmermann remains transparent on her website that she creates the cakes in her home kitchen. "I find that people respond very positively to my home-based business," Zimmermann adds. "In today's world with big commercial, industrial operations, folks like seeing exactly where their cake will be made and know who is making it."

"Custom, handmade cakes are my specialty," shares Zimmermann. "Each cake I design is a unique creation. ... I don't have mass-produced stock cake designs out of a book like grocery stores and many other bakeries where you select a number, such as A13 or B12, and they just duplicate the picture. Each cake we design is a unique creation." She does nearly all of the work herself, making over ninety cakes a year. Zimmermann prides herself in a strong working relationship with her clients to custom-design each cake, which can involve custom matching the colors to swatches supplied by their clients. "No pre-made bakery mint greens or bubblegum pinks here."

Name: Suzy Zimmermann

Business: Queen of Cake and Events

Website: Queen-of-Cake.com

Products: specialty decorated cakes; wedding cakes

Sales Venue: individual custom order

Annual Sales: nearing $50,000 gross sales cap

Suzy Zimmermann of Queen of Cake and Events creates all of the lavish details and decorations for her cakes by hand. CONSTANTE PHOTO

"People often can't understand how our cakes can take so long to make and why the price can be higher as a result," she explains. The creation time for a Queen of Cake creation can range from eighteen to sixty hours.

"Contrary to what you see on the ever-growing countless number of television cake shows, custom cake making takes time," shares Zimmermann. "Everything I do is by hand, from gilding edible gold leaves to hand-cutting stencils to match patterns from an invitation or fabrics. Some decorative items like our bows, bow loops, gum paste flowers, sugar monograms and hand-sculpted figures are all created in-house two to three weeks in advance to ensure ample drying time."

For these reasons, Zimmermann asks clients to place their orders as far in advance as possible (up to eighteen months) and requires them to come in for a private consultation to ensure everything comes out just how they want it. Customers pay a non-refundable seventy-five dollars for this consultation, which is applied to the final cake price if they end up ordering. For estimating purposes, Queen of Cake creations average $3.25 per person for a basic, minimally decorated cake, with prices going up based on customization.

Zimmermann diversified her business in 2012 to include event planning. Now officially "Queen of Cake and Events," Zimmermann can also handle everything from flowers to decorations to music. "Event planning proved to be a natural fit to the cake business as I was quite familiar with the ins and outs of wedding and other party logistics and tend to be a very detailed-orientated person."

Each Queen of Cake creation is custom designed for the individual wedding client and can take up to sixty hours to produce.

<small>CONSTANTE PHOTO</small>

"Remember cake decorating is an art form that always evolves and changes, so it's important to keep up on the trends," adds Zimmermann. Most major cities have a local cake club (Zimmermann is serving for a second term as president of hers) that she recommends as a resource as well as joining the International Cake Exploration Society (ICES; ices.org) to learn about what's new. Currently, Zimmermann sees a lot of use of metallic in cake decorating as well as edible wafer paper used to create decorations like edible flowers. "I thrive on and love the newness and challenge of constantly creating new cake designs, but the most rewarding part is the ongoing relationships with the bride and her family in developing her dream design. My clients become part of my extended family."

As Zimmermann's business success grows and she nears the $50,000 gross sales cap limit under Texas cottage food law, she finds herself at a crossroad in determining the next step for her venture. "I hate to turn away business, but on the flip side I really don't want a commercial bakery. I absolutely love my arrangement and working from home."

That "do what you love" message rings true when Zimmermann offers advice to budding cottage food entrepreneurs: "Be true to who you are," she shares. "Find out what you love doing, whether it's cookies or sheet cakes or the kind of wedding specialty cakes I do, and stick with that. Your love and passion for your end product will show; don't try to be like everyone else."

Cooling on a counter, biscotti to be sold at a holiday bazaar. JOHN D. IVANKO

need to go through a more involved home kitchen inspection and licensing process, plus meet a host of other requirements specified by the retailers or distributors themselves, like having UPC codes for all of your products. Depending on your wholesale client, you may need to guarantee production and regular delivery of a certain quantity of product that, of course, meets impeccable quality and consistency standards. More about this in the final section of the book.

Mail Order

The vast majority of states with cottage food laws do not allow mail order, either within their own state or across state borders. However, a few states with broader "home processor licenses" allow products to be sold wholesale as well as mail order. Be certain to clarify if mail order refers to within your state or nationally.

Stay on Target for a Bull's-eye

While the enthusiasm might be there to pursue more than one of the sales venues detailed above, we caution against it, at least when just starting up. It's best to begin by targeting the venue with the highest probability of strong sales and repeat customers, to establish your business within your financial and time limitations. You can always expand later, once you have a track record and firm footing.

There are many ways to approach each and every topic covered in this book. You'll need to evaluate which make the most sense to you, your situation, budget, goals and, of course, your state's cottage food law.

7

Promotion: Persuading Customers with Advertising and Public Relations

I F THE TARGET AUDIENCE FOR YOUR PRODUCTS happens to be your neighbors, family or co-workers eagerly awaiting your kitchen creations, then produce, package and deliver your product and let the money roll in as you keep them stocked and happy.

For most food entrepreneurs, however, you'll need to let potential customers know your company exists to serve their needs with products you've tested and know they'll love. You'll need to reach out to connect with these potential customers, whether they're in your office, school, church or neighborhood.

You need not empty the bank to promote your product, however. Depending on your skill set, comfort with a computer, time and budget, there are many free or nearly free promotional opportunities covered in this chapter. Despite the saying, "you have to spend money to make money," we've found that the less you have to spend in promotion, the more you earn selling your products. The trick is to find the most cost-effective way to reach your target market.

Promotion

Promotion is what most of us think about as marketing, the applied art form of persuasive communication by graphics, words and such to help sell products. Creative, innovative thinking thrives through your approach to promotion, communicating information — telling the story about your product — that leads to customers wanting to buy your products. Promotion helps them realize they have a need that will be satisfied by purchasing your product.

Marketers often refer to brand as the embodiment of your product in the form of your name, logo and other design aspects. The goal, of course, is to devise communications that help your customers understand and remember what your business is about and why they'll love your products. While multinational corporations spend millions on developing their brand, you can do it with almost no money at all by harnessing the power of the Internet and a home computer, plus your own creativity.

Included in promotion is both advertising and public relations (PR). Advertising is purchased while PR, whether solicited or unsolicited, is free. The smaller the business, the less you'll need to focus on paying for traditional advertising in media like magazines or newspapers and the more you might want to focus on public relations efforts, since PR involves investing time, not money.

Promotion decisions include developing a sense of what your company offers with words, graphics and other communicative elements. These elements often include your logo, product slogan and unifying colors, styles, themes and images expressing what you do, for whom and why it matters. They position your product in the marketplace.

Advertising

In the traditional sense, advertising is paid forms of communication via outlets such as newspapers, magazines, TV and radio. Depending on what products you're selling and your existing networks of friends, community connections and comfort with a computer and the Internet, most of your promotional efforts can be accomplished by spending little to nothing on traditional paid advertising. Save your money and focus on Internet communications and PR instead.

However, don't rule out the possibility of exchanging your products for a display advertisement in a newspaper. Publications, particularly regional or non-profit newsletters, may be open to creating a giveaway of your product (perhaps as an incentive for renewals) in exchange for a "free" publication advertisement, which will garner you conventional advertising exposure through an unconventional means. So if you get a local newspaper sales call, float the idea by them as a marketing promotion.

Posters and Flyers

For most CFOs, if you're planning to spend anything on advertising, it will be on a printed flyer to pass around to your neighbors or co-workers, a poster to be displayed at the local library and other public places, and maybe a few nicely crafted letters to area businesses or organizations announcing your new venture, with a product order form attached (and, if appropriate, some samples in a box).

How you advertise will be predicated on what you're selling and how, based on your state laws. On this book's website, we share a few examples as a guide. Don't leave out contact information, any order specifics (like minimum orders) and whether or not free delivery is included.

Direct Marketing

In the same way many CFOs sell their products directly to their customers, direct marketing connects your messages directly to those you wish to reach. While social media can be viewed as direct marketing, there are many other channels used to elicit direct responses from potential customers. Some of the most widely used include promotional letters, newsletters and postcards, sent via mail, e-mail or text messaging.

- **Mail**

  Most of us are familiar with catalogs and credit card offers delivered to us via the US Postal Service. While they're becoming less common thanks to the exploding use of electronic forms of communication, sending a polished "snail mail" letter, perhaps with a coupon to sample your product, to potential customers can be effective, particularly if you are trying to land a large account like a weekly bakery order for an office. But you need to reach the right decision-maker or your solicitation letter may end up with the rest of the "junk mail." You may need to make a few "cold calls" to receptionists or secretaries first, before you send out your sampler pack and introductory letter. On a national level, an entire industry represented by the Direct Marketing Association (the-dma.org) serves companies that assemble direct mail databases used to solicit business.

- **E-mail List Campaigns**

  Like catalogs in the mail, spam in our in-box has become an accepted, albeit unwanted, aspect of having e-mail, the electronic form of direct communication via the Internet. With the widespread availability of free e-mail, more people than ever have adopted this means of both receiving and sending messages.

Besides crafting simple e-mails that announce a new product or event you will be selling at, you can also design more sophisticated e-mails using graphically rich templates from many e-mail systems, perhaps ones you already use.

You may, however, encounter a limit as to how many e-mails you can send out at one time — in part, an (unsuccessful) effort by technology companies to curb spam. So if you have a large enough database of names, you may find yourself needing to use various free or low cost e-mail management systems, plus a host of other marketing features. Among some of the most widely used service providers are MailChimp (mailchimp.com), Constant Contact (constantcontact.com) and Emma (myemma.com). Besides price, each e-mail service provider may offer various analytics and other customizable options and design features.

A word of caution, however. Like "junk mail," keep what you e-mail out relevant, helpful and informative, otherwise you run the risk of turning off the very customers you want to excite and engage. If you send too many messages, too often, you run the risk of turning constant contact into a constant annoyance.

Websites

One of the easiest ways to raise awareness and establish a degree of professionalism around your product and company is to create a website. This digital presence allows you to share information about your company and what you produce. For whatever reasons, a few states' cottage food laws prohibit any Internet-based advertising or communication; double-check to make sure this restriction doesn't apply to you. Even if your state forbids sales via the Internet, you can still have a website to share general product and company information and take an order over the telephone.

On the website would, of course, be your company name, products, contact information, order forms (if allowed in your state) and a backstory that explains what you're all about. While there are lots of opinions about what makes a great website, ease of navigation remains important. Most websites have either a navigation bar across the top or along one side, containing words or a graphic that connects you to key components, or pages, on the site.

Be sure to include a slice of your personal story. This helps differentiate your products from the mass-produced ones on the supermarket shelves. A simple "About" page could include a photo of you in the kitchen preparing your products, plus a lively question and answer format that helps support and promote your story. Replies to the following questions may be a great place to start:

- How did you get started making your product?
- What makes your product unique?
- Why did you start (your business name)?
- When you're not in the kitchen, what are you doing?

Another important feature may be a "frequently asked questions," or FAQ, page. This page can deflect time-consuming telephone or e-mail questions and clarify your policies and procedures. Included might be answers to the following questions:

- How can I get your product?
- Do you have a minimum order?
- Can you deliver?
- What kind of payment do you accept?
- How quick is your turnaround on an order?

The graphics, style and feel of your website should echo your products in terms of the design, color schemes and other creative elements. For example, if you decide to use a red-checked gingham pattern for your products, this could be cleverly worked into the design of the website as well. Featuring customer endorsements, testimonials or any media coverage you may have received will help reinforce the quality of your products and the reputation of your company.

Thanks to "widgets," self-contained mini programs you just paste into sections of your website, you can keep your homepage dynamic and fresh with new content that gets posted to there, perhaps via a social media update. Feedburner (feedburner.com) is a tool that can be used to automatically repost your social media post to your website page.

There are two ways to approach a website for your business, one which involves money and another that is completely free. Gone are the days when you needed big bucks for a website. Since many cottage food businesses may be just getting off the ground, starting with a free website might be the simplest and wisest choice.

1. Free Websites

The following companies offer the ability to modify easy-to-use templates and customize them for your business; there are many other options as well. If you have some computer experience, the intuitive nature of the websites make them easy to navigate, and instructional videos will guide you through the design, so there's no programming or "coding" involved. The websites do have some space and creative limitations and may come with small ads that also appear on your website. But for most first-timers, you'll be amazed by the results. Just register for the website template you like the best and start uploading text and photos. There's plenty of free storage space.

- **wordpress.com**

  It's so easy an eleven-year-old can do it. Really. This is the leading blogging interface that can be adapted easily as a business website. For the record, "blog" stands for a "web log." If you love writing about your products, ingredients or journey as a food entrepreneur, this option will be particularly attractive.

- **wix.com**

  Containing numerous templates, many product oriented, this online website builder focuses on easy drag-and-drop design elements. Stick to their HTML5 options, since more and more people are viewing websites via their mobile smartphones, so you want to make sure your website looks okay on these tiny devices, too.

- **weebly.com**

  A very basic, visuals-driven website design interface. Not many bells and whistles, but its simplicity will appeal to less tech-savvy people and get you quickly set up on the Internet.

- **sites.google.com**
  Created by the most widely used Internet search engine company, Google Sites provides the ability to create a free website with various features. If you like to write regularly, then you can use Google's blogspot.com.

2. Low-cost Websites

More experienced entrepreneurs who want greater control over their name, products, design elements and capabilities can purchase their domain name (the name you select to represent your company) and then host their own website. Both the domain name and hosting fees cost less than $100 per year from companies like GoDaddy.com.

Hosting and designing your own website may require greater computer knowledge than you have the time or interest for. If so, you could hire a website designer depending on your budget, your design goals and the scope of what you want the website to do for your business. Some CFOs find a family member, friend or neighbor happy to help design a professional-looking website, perhaps in exchange for a regular supply of cookies or jams.

Social Media

Everything you do is about sharing your story. Don't overlook ways to let your customers do this for you as well. To build awareness around your product, you'll need to get people to try it, love it and share what they like about it with the rest of the world. With the explosive growth of the Internet — plus access to it through computers, mobile phones and tablets — social media have become an increasingly important part of an advertising campaign. And it need not cost you a penny to get started.

Your most effective advertising are the satisfied customers themselves. Word of mouth has always trumped a four-color display ad in a magazine. People are much more likely to trust their friends than a company trying to sell them something (even if what you're selling is really great).

Thanks to the proliferation of social media, there are lots of options for sharing your story with the world, in characters, updates, photos and video. The multiplier-effect cannot be overstated. But it does require a different modus operandi, where talking becomes typing and a printed poster becomes a "folder" of incredible photos of your products, your home kitchen and your customers savoring a bite of what you've produced. Because there aren't enough hours in the day to do them all, carefully select the social media your customers use most.

The more your customers rave about your products to others on the Internet, the better. People who love your product can, in spirit, be your "in-house" advertising agency. They can tell their friends, share links to your products on Facebook and tweet about their favorites, too.

Facebook: facebook.com

Currently, the dominant social media networking service, where you can keep connected to your customers and share regular social updates, such as a new product or an event you'll be selling at next week. As part of their marketing strategy, some companies are now choosing to make their business Facebook page their de facto "website."

When you start your Facebook page for your venture, be sure to select and create a "business" profile, not a "personal" page. This keeps your business professional and opens up opportunities you won't have on your personal page, including the ability to schedule posts in advance, assign other people as administrators (to help you), access analytic tools and implement targeted advertising campaigns, if you choose to do so down the line.

Google+: google.com/+/business

This search engine giant likewise has ambitions to thrive in the social media world through Google-plus for business.

Twitter: twitter.com

If you like texting, then this online microblogging website is perfect for sharing what's happening with your business in 140 characters or less.

Pinterest: pinterest.com

Think cork bulletin board with photos, embedded on an Internet page. This pinboard-style website can spread images of your food products through the Internet if your photos are beautiful enough.

Instagram: instagram.com

Like Twitter, except what you share is snapshots, not text. So when your product wins a state fair or is enjoyed by your state governor, share that candid photo here. Instagram currently only works with mobile devices.

Spirit Cake Sales Pour in via Social Media

When most folks go on a Caribbean cruise, they come home with a tan. Rhonda L. Jones came back with a dream of launching a rum cake business from her home kitchen.

"At the last minute I ended up going on a cruise to the Grand Cayman Islands when a family member was unable to go," shares Jones. "Onboard, I went to a rum tasting and a later excursion to a local rum cake bakery when we docked. I brought back a few bottles of duty-free rum and started recipe experimenting with my family as taste-testers until I nailed it." With this distinct recipe in her kitchen repertoire, Jones embraced the opportunity to launch a bakery business.

"My passion for baking started early in life; I remember baking my dad miniature pineapple layer cakes in my Easy Bake Oven," Jones recalls. "I grew up in a household that loved sharing food. My mother baked every chance she found, and I helped at her side making her specialties of apple pies, peach cobbler and yeast rolls. I never realized back then that those experiences would so directly impact me today."

Jones' business roots are in people and creating connections through the kitchen. Everything is personal with a story behind it, starting with the name of her business: Chez Moi. "I simply love the French language, which started with my dad teaching me words and phrases when I was very young. I continued learning French by studying it in high school and lived in Boug-en-Bresse in France my junior year. Folks might initially think I do French pastries. But it's the meaning of Chez Moi that inspired the name: 'My Place.' As I work under a home processor license administered by the North Carolina Department of Agriculture, that name reflects me on an even deeper level."

North Carolina is one of the states with an expanded approach

Name: Rhonda L. Jones

Business: Chez Moi Bakery (Durham, North Carolina)

Website: iloverumcake.com

Products: spirit and plain cakes, ice cream cakewiches and panna cotta with homemade dessert sauces

Sales Venue: direct, mail order, special events, food truck

Annual Sales: $30,000

Chez Moi Bakery owner Rhonda Jones inside her food truck, which she uses to deliver and sell her cakes.
COURTESY OF JONES FAMILY

to home-based food operations. Her home processor license allows Jones to sell a broad array of products via outlets such as mail order, wholesale and her most recent venture: a food truck.

"The initial inspection and licensing process took a little time. But once I went through that, I've had a lot of flexibility, along with support from our department of agriculture, on growing and diversifying my business."

Jones' focus on rum and other spirit cakes came out of a clear understanding that she needed to differentiate her products. "To truly shine, you need to drill down to what you're good at making and make sure it is something unique and not already offered. With a saturated cupcake market here in Durham, I saw opportunity in rum cakes."

After launching in 2005, Jones focused strictly on holiday sales of rum cakes for the first five years. "Rum cakes fit well with the Christmas season. Even though it is distinctly different than a fruit cake, folks still associate rum cakes as something similar and a special holiday treat," adds Jones. In year two, she pumped out orders for forty rum cakes. She then added two additional ovens to keep up with the volume.

Today Jones sells rum cakes year-round, primarily through direct and mail order along with a couple of wholesale accounts. For example, Cocoa Cinnamon, a local coffeehouse, sells her cakes by the slice. Chez Moi offers tempting twists on spirit cakes, which sell for twenty and thirty-five dollars in small and large sizes. In addition to her signature flavor, brown sugar vanilla classic rum cake, she offers ten other varieties, like black cherry bourbon and apple martini.

Chez Moi Bakery's rum cake on display.
Courtesy of Chez Moi Bakery

Jones advises other start-ups to focus on your key unique products and not try to do too much. She learned this herself. "At first I offered both the spirit cakes and what I called 'Timeless Classics,' cakes like carrot, red velvet and chocolate layer. That second holiday season I had forty rum cake orders and one carrot cake. I quickly realized my niche."

Jones finds social media, particularly Twitter, her main marketing outlet. "Social media creates a personal connection between my customers and me. Best of all, it's free," she explains. "By tweeting anything, from where our food truck will be next to photos from my recent trip to Europe, it shows that I'm the face behind Chez Moi and folks feel connected to me." She posts her tweets using various key hashtags that link with the right audience interested in local, unique food such as #Foodie, #BuyLocal, #GoDurham, #Entrepreneur and #DurhamIsTastiest. Social media and word of mouth are her number one sources of new customers.

Rhonda Jones with a labeled cake box.
COURTESY OF COCOA CINNAMON

"I try to post at least a few times a week and then, again, a few times while I am at an event with the dessert truck, then focusing primarily on where I'll be and what I'm serving," shares Jones. "Some people say more is better, but I prefer quality over quantity when it comes to posts. I re-Tweet others, especially other food trucks, and share photos of new items." Jones sees Twitter and Facebook as serving two different purposes, with Facebook serving more like a website with easy-to-access, permanent information and Twitter more for instant and immediate updates such as the food truck location.

In 2013, Jones further diversified by investing in a food truck and selling both sliced cake and ice cream "cakewiches" made with her spirit cakes at local events. This enabled her to strategically expand the business by diversifying her customer base. The ability to sell cake by the slice introduced Jones' product to new customers who wouldn't commit to buying a full cake before they tried it. The ice cream cakewiches, using alcohol-infused cake, gave foodies a new, exciting dessert treat.

"Because I do all the baking and assembly in my kitchen, I could save money as I didn't need an expensive food truck with a full mobile kitchen. I just needed a mobile unit for sales and could use a redesigned van instead," explains Jones.

She raised the $3,290 toward the purchase of this unit via a Kickstarter campaign (see Chapter 15 for more on Kickstarter). "Crowdfunding seems to work best when your company has been selling a product for a while and has an established, loyal base. I know some other local businesses which have raised over $20,000."

"The incredible support of my friends, family and the Durham community keeps me going and growing Chez Moi," Jones adds. While she currently runs the business as a sole proprietor, friends help with the larger

events when she needs an extra hand as cashier and are "paid" in cake and appreciation. Jones currently manages Chez Moi while still holding down a full-time day job in conference planning and is training someone to run the food truck while she's at that other job. But she's working on her vision of making this a full-time gig. "For me to transition full-time, I want to diversify and supplement my income with a shelf-stable product, a cake mix specifically made for folks who want to make these spirit cakes in their own kitchen and sauces which can be added to any dessert."

In the meantime, Jones keeps her local customers stocked with cakes — and happy. "Connecting with my customers is the best part of this business," Jones sums up. "I love to see them take the first bite and enjoy their Chez Moi experience."

YouTube: youtube.com

A free, movie-sharing website, particularly useful if you have the talent and interest in creating videos around your products and their use in the kitchen, perhaps as cooking demos.

LinkedIn: linkedin.com

This professional business network can connect you to people once impossible to reach, if you can get into their inner business circle. It's all about degrees — or links — of separation. Try it out and see if you're only six degrees of separation away from everyone you might want to meet.

Just because you have 742 Facebook "friends" doesn't mean these friends see every "status update" you post. Make no mistake, not only are Facebook and other social media sites mining personal information about you and your online life, they're making money off you, too. In fact, if you have your "cookies" disabled on your browser, you cannot even sign in to use the site; cookies track everything you do. Facebook and many other social media companies have proprietary and secret algorithms they use to control how many people see your updates.

If you want to boost your reach and increase your audience on social media, you have to pay for it. This is called "pay-for-clicks." You can focus on people who like your page and their friends, or broaden your reach to people you target. Right on their main business page, the social media site will show you how you can increase your reach and how much it will cost you; heck, they even create a sample advertisement out of the content you just provided.

All you have to do is enter your credit card and set your parameters, including your budget, target market and duration of the campaign. Then with a click of a button, your ad will reach a segment of the population so specific that it's a bit creepy, at least to us. The good news, however, is you can effectively target a market at a potentially very low cost; your update will show up in their "news feed."

Listing on Free Directories

While most cottage food businesses can't sell by mail or cross state lines, getting listed on one or more of the many free national Internet directories can help locals find you. This will also be another means for media to access your information.

Forrager: forrager.com
It's billed as the "cottage food community," a space where home cooks, bakers and decorators can learn and share with each other. Solely focused on the cottage food industry, Forrager has grown from an information portal into an online community, where people can ask and answer questions, connect with each other, and add their cottage food operation to the directory.

Etsy: etsy.com
An e-commerce website developed to sell handmade items. There are only a few food product companies listed, perhaps due to laws that restrict online sales.

LocalHarvest: localharvest.org
Only for farms with food products for sale.

Agrilicious: agrilicious.com
For all things local food, connecting potential customers, farmers and food-related businesses.

Eat Well Guide: eatwellguide.org
Go to "suggest a listing" and suggest your company and its products.

CSA Center: csacenter.org
Only for farms operating with the community supported agriculture model (Robyn Van En Center).

All Organic Links: allorganiclinks.com
For various organic products.

Product Demonstrations and Sampling

Sampling out your product, whether on the table at a farmers' market or in a "sampler box" you give a prospective company that hosts regular morning roll days or birthday gatherings for employees, is an effective way to get potential customers to try it without any financial commitment on their part. If your items taste as good as your market feasibility studies suggest, then you're just an order form away from landing a new customer.

Every happy customer can lead to two or more down the line. Most catering and cake decorating companies, for example, thrive off referrals. It may take months, or even years, to build this buzz, but once it happens, the work you'll have to do marketing your business will be greatly reduced, depending on the sales goals that you've set for yourself. Remember to thank those loyal and supportive customers, perhaps with special gifts during the holidays or discounts with every referral they send your way.

Public Relations

PR represents your reputation and brand image. It's what both you and the public say about your business or product. Securing solicited or unsolicited

Samples Anyone? A Word of Caution

If where you sell offers the possibility of sampling your product, that's one of the best ways to clinch a sale. But thanks to numerous regulations and requirements, you may find this more problematic and a hassle than it's worth.

At many farmers' markets around the country, trolling health inspectors have effectively put the kibosh on sampling out products because of fears of food spoilage, customers contaminating the samples or on other grounds. You'll need to check with the individual venue to see what their specific rules are. You may be required, for example, to serve samples wearing food service-grade disposable gloves. Check with other vendors, too, since they can tip you off if the market or craft fair, for whatever reasons, is on the watch list for the health department.

HeathGlen's Farm & Kitchen products with single-use sampling spoons.
Courtesy of HeathGlen's
Farm & Kitchen

media coverage can be far more cost effective than any paid display advertisement or classified ad.

By sharing your product story effectively and strategically with various media outlets through a PR campaign, you will:

- Increase visibility of your products and business
- Add credibility to your operations
- Enhance your image
- Sell more products without having to spend a cent
- Create more interest in a "buy local" movement and economy

Ways to Generate Media Coverage

Everyone's business and food products could make a great topic for an article. But what's your hook and news angle to get free media coverage? The

Hosting Private Product Parties

If your state permits it, another option may be to host a private "product party" along the lines of a Pampered Chef or Tupperware gathering. Invite over your friends, neighbors and other community members in your target market for a private party to taste your products and learn more about how you make them. If you make the event an invitation-only private party, you may sidestep legal regulations; the health department, for instance, should only concern themselves with public events where food is sold or served. Private is the key word.

This unique format could welcome people into your home kitchen to see where and how you make your products. Besides sampling, you might offer suggestions on hosting a brunch based around your products or pairing them with others. You could do a blind tasting to get people talking about how your product is better. Such parties can be ripe for testimonials, provide new product ideas and create a buzz in social media. Everyone likes being invited to a party, especially if the food is homemade and delicious — and free.

You may want to generate press clippings, gather endorsements, collect testimonials or grow your customer base. If you cast the net wide enough to include invitations to some local newspaper reporters, it's possible they will create a news story about you and your new products (covered in the PR section of this chapter). To make your private product party more newsworthy, tie it to national event, like Bake Cookies Day in December (if you're a baker) or "Canvolution," organized by Canning Across America (if you're a canner or have your own line of pickles).

following ten steps will help increase the likelihood of receiving the media exposure you deserve.

Step 1: Identify your media goals

In addition to increasing awareness of your products and business, what specifically do you want to accomplish with your PR campaign? You may want to generate press clippings, gather endorsements, collect testimonials or grow your customer base. For example, do you want to introduce a new product or invite your community to a product demo party event?

Step 2: Create your compelling story

Identify your strengths, unique characteristics and what makes your products and background special. Keep your story simple and describe it as if you're talking with a friend.

Step 3: Develop a media list

Compile a list of media contacts, including the names of writers, journalists or producers who regularly cover related topics. Start a file of articles published or aired by those journalists, since this might be a way to make an initial contact. If you have the time and inclination, build relationships with journalists before you pitch your first story idea. Thanks to LinkedIn, Twitter and Facebook, this is easier than ever before. When contacting someone, it often helps to tell them how much you enjoyed a story they wrote or produced.

Step 4: Write a press release

Follow the standard press release format. See the sample press kit on this book's website (homemade forsale.com) for a downloadable template.

Win Some Awards

You know you have a great-tasting product, and your current customers do, too. But to reach new customers and grow your business and reputation, there's nothing like winning an award for your pickle relish or artisanal sourdough bread. Whether it's a "People's Choice" award, a state fair ribbon or a prestigious Good Food Award (goodfoodawards.org) from Seedling Projects, such an accolade can boost your reputation and solidify your position as a leader with a third-party endorsement. It will also allow you to add "award-winning" to your marketing materials and may even include attractive medals you can use in your market displays. Depending on the nature of the award and the fame associated with it, you may also attract media attention and new customers eager to try out the next great food product.

Step 5: Capture visuals, both photographs and video

A picture is worth a thousand words, it's often said. Don't miss an opportunity to share your story visually. High-quality digital single-lens reflex (SLR) and GoPro video cameras make taking great shots a breeze. Make sure you capture images at a high resolution so they can be used in print or even on TV. With photos or video, you can turn a small mention into a larger feature or product profile. Shrinking budgets at various media with limited photography capability may allow you to showcase your story more effectively. Visual content is in demand more than ever, by magazines, newspapers and even the Associated Press. Plus, you can capture the images you want, presenting your products in the best light.

Step 6: Time your press release

Most magazines work ahead from three to six months (or more) when covering a story. Newspapers work a week ahead. Don't forget about local radio, since people interact with the media in many ways; those who watch lots of TV may not regularly listen to the radio. Internet media, like food bloggers, are always eager to cover stories and enjoy passing out free samples to their readers; plus, their blogs can sometimes go viral, which means what they write gets picked up, over and over again, by other bloggers.

Step 7: Submit your release

E-mail your release to a specific person or media contact, then follow up with a telephone call or e-mail about one or two weeks later to make sure they received it. Ask the assignment editor, producer or journalist if the story has been "assigned," or if it's still being reviewed. While targeting major outlets, focus on the media you believe you have the best chance of reaching; perhaps these media cover topics related to your products or regularly include "human interest" features.

Step 8: Accept and manage the interview (and photography session)

The interview or meeting can be the most enjoyable part of working with the media. Relax and just be you. Your enthusiasm will carry the interview, but make sure you share your story about your products. Avoid "going off the record" about anything and minimize detailed or complex issues. A little warm hospitality goes a long way with journalists; send them home with some of your product.

Step 9: Offer thanks for the media coverage

After an article or story has run or aired, send a thank you note and keep in touch as future story ideas arise.

Step 10: Keep track of it all

Keep a list with links of media articles about your products and your business. An easy way to do this is to set up a free "Google Alert" via Google with your name and the name of your products and business. Google will send you a link via e-mail every time they track something with your name in it. Set up an alert here: google.com/alert. Once you've received a glowing review or business profile, don't let it stop there. Share the media article or coverage on your website or via social media, making sure to tag the writer or media source using the @ or # sign, depending on the social media, so it shows up on their social media page.

8

People, Partnerships and Purpose

THANKS TO A FRAGMENTED MARKETPLACE and the advent of powerful new technologies, marketing is playing an increasingly important role in the success of a product. Besides the traditional 4 Ps of marketing covered previously, we added three Ps to address the growing importance of People, Partnerships and Purpose in the success of your marketing efforts.

People

One way or another, your food product will satisfy some need of your customers in a delicious way. The need could be for a convenient and tasty snack at an event or an attractive Valentine's Day tin of heart-shaped, hand-dipped chocolate pralines. People are people, but how you determine whether they're customers or consumers can improve your bottom line. Are they enjoying your product themselves or sharing it with someone they love? Are they interested in the taste alone or the experience they have enjoying it?

Customers Versus Consumers

When you're defining your target market, you may notice that sometimes the person buying your product is different from the person eating it. In marketing circles, we talk about decision-makers as well as decision-influencers. Take kids and their parents, for example. Who has more pull when it comes to that jar of jelly on the shelf, or type of cookie in the cookie jar?

A mother may be the decision-maker with the bucks to buy a loaf of your healthy, whole-grain bread to make sandwiches for her family that week. She might also be the parent who breaks down at an arts and crafts fair and picks up your decorated cookies after being nagged by her hungry kids. It may be the husband, however, who seeks out an anniversary treat

he and his wife can share together. Or a customer may, on impulse, pick up a gift on their holiday trip that they couldn't pass up — perhaps due to your sampling efforts, slick packaging or catchy name. This could be a gift for themselves or for a friend back home who has been walking their dog during their vacation.

When thinking about who might buy your product, decide whether you are going to target the customers with the cash or the consumers who actually end up savoring it. Your marketing can be designed to reach one or both of these audiences, albeit with different messages and goals in mind. Back to that jelly example: the kids need to know that your brand of jelly tastes great on a PB and J, but Mom or Dad (whomever gets the groceries in the house) needs to know that yours is made with local, organic fruit and has no artificial colors or flavors.

As we cover in the Scaling Up section of this book, when you're selling wholesale, this customer-consumer dichotomy becomes even more complex. In some cases, you may be two or three layers removed from the end consumers of your products. You may be selling first to a food broker, distributor and/or retailer before your product is purchased at retail. Each of these layers has industry standards — and pricing demands — which must be met.

Products or Experiences?

You determine the experience your customers may have with your product. Interactions with customers move beyond "transactional" relationships, seeking to establish unique, emotional and uncommon experiences for individual customers. Your product has the potential to be so much more than merely an exchange of money for a cupcake. The marketing research firm Strategic Horizons, founded by Joseph Pine and Jim Gilmore, examine this idea in their book *The Experience Economy: Work Is Theatre and Every Business Is a Stage*, where they write, "experiences are as distinct from services as services are from goods."

With cottage food products, this thinking involves creating an experience around the enjoyment of your product and not simply focusing on its attributes, such as taste, flavor or size. Adding an experiential dimension of your product is another way to differentiate it in the marketplace and connect you on a relational level with those who enjoy eating what you love making.

"The New Artisan Economy has become hotter than hot in our cities. This trend is especially visible in the form of new, small-scale companies focusing on local craftsmanship. Consumers are more and more demanding for local products that are produced in a sustainable way, with care for the environment. Keywords in the New Artisan Economy are local, authentic and sustainable. One thing the companies of the New Artisan Economy have in common are the strong stories that come with their products."

— Ted Pouls, PopUpCity.net

Next time you visit a farmers' market, notice the relationships and bonds between farmers and their customers, who will eat the food they grow. Your booth selling pickles, preserves or freshly baked products extends this local economy and naturally thrives there. Many who frequent farmers' markets are there for the friendship, the ecological connections to the land and a sense of hope and optimism for the future — far more than for the potatoes, peapods or your homemade salsa. What you're selling is adding to this richness of community.

As well as being a neighbor, a colleague at the office or a familiar face at your local YMCA, you're many people's personal connection to the local economy. You complete the growing interest in "buying local" by selling local. The trust and respect you earn from the relationships with your customers differentiate your products from the made-from-mixes, mass-produced or factory-generated products made somewhere far, far away.

Taking Care of Customers

Taking care of your customers is part of the experience you create around your product. Maintaining a high level of customer service is the best thing you have going for your business, leading to word-of-mouth endorsements and referrals. Regardless of the product you sell, building relationships with your customers demands a few key ingredients:

- Selling a great-tasting product at a fair price;
- Promotional efforts that are honest, authentic and never misleading;
- Professional and courteous service, with on-time deliveries;
- Accurate invoicing and billing;
- Extending some form of thanks for every referral, Tweet or "Like" on Facebook;
- Taking any criticism or feedback constructively, never personally.

The more you can deliver every order with a smile, the better. Never lose sight: you're the face of the food.

The 80–20 Rule

From the first telephone call to the delivery of a product, how you interact and form relationships with your customers solidify your position in the

"Your creations are experienced on a visceral level; your passion comes across in every bite. More than musicians, more than writers, you live the virtues of authenticity, passion, community and connection. Every food crafter has by necessity created a tight-knit community around them. Your work is a true and authentic expression of tradition. And like any good artist, you walk this path not for the promise of a pot of gold at the end, but from a drive to express what is deep inside you."

— Sarah Weiner, Founder of the Good Food Awards (goodfoodawards.org), addressing the 2014 Winners

market. Many companies or organizations we've consulted for or interviewed use the 80–20 rule to help prioritize their marketing efforts and focus on building long-term relationships and loyalty among a select group of customers.

Practical experience has led many business owners to observe that about 80 percent of their sales come from only 20 percent of their customers. Covet the 20 percent and do everything possible to keep them

Maintaining a Customer Database

Every business must both attract customers and retain customers. Once you have customers, maintaining records about them can help you sustain and grow your enterprise. From tracking your customer orders and preferences to capturing useful information like birth dates and anniversaries for relationship-building marketing efforts, your customer database serves as the fuel to propel your business. Without customers, you won't be in business for long.

Keeping written records of important customer details in a notebook or on index cards has increasingly given way to various computer or electronic-based programs or systems. Among the simplest is a spreadsheet, like Microsoft's Excel program, where you can list contact information, orders, anniversary dates, customer referrals, frequency of orders and product preferences, among other details.

While it used to be very expensive to take it up a notch with a custom-designed customer database that could be linked to direct marketing efforts as well as invoicing and bookkeeping functions, there are now numerous, low-cost e-mail marketing services available that may work well for your purposes, both for e-mail marketing and as a customer database. Among these are Emma, Constant Contact and MailChimp, covered in the previous chapter.

Some computer operating systems, like Apple's Mail program included in their OS X for a MacBook Pro, include a basic database program sophisticated enough that you can record contact details, key order information and customer likes and dislikes, plus send out e-mail newsletters. Apple's Mail program comes with a few sample newsletter templates that you can easily customize with your photos; additional templates can be purchased. You may be limited by your hosting service or local Internet service provider, however, in terms of how many e-mails can be sent out at one time; it's their strategy to deter spamming. For example, we can only send out batches of 100 e-mailed newsletters at a time.

In today's world of identity theft and privacy concerns, be attuned to your customers' requests and make sure the data you collect is secure. Keeping credit cards numbers or check information on file electronically seems to be a disaster waiting to happen. And avoid selling your customer information to any third party, since you run the risk of violating your customers' trust in you and your business.

happy, since they're the ones that are repeat customers or big on referrals. If you host special tasting events, make sure they're on your VIP list. If you carefully manage your customer database and can keep track of birthdays and anniversaries, send a congratulatory note or small food gift.

In part due to your relationships with your customers, you can help them help you. As discussed previously, customer referrals remain the most powerful form of unpaid advertising or public relations. The words of a satisfied customer craft a long-lasting message about you and the reputation of your company and its products. Don't hesitate to ask enthusiastic customers for an endorsement quote to use on your brochure or website; don't be surprised when many blog about you.

Never underestimate a personal touch in communicating with your customers. A handwritten thank-you note to a customer who referred a friend adds a lasting impact for the price of a stamp. In our world of rapid technology and e-mails possibly lost in a flurry of spam, a personal touch can go a long way.

Collaborators and Vendors

When we talk about People in promotion, we're not just talking about reaching customers. There may be aspects of your business where you need assistance, like graphic design, website development, public relations or with your computer. While you could hire people or companies to help you take on various projects, some of these individuals may want to collaborate with you in exchange for the products you create. Addressed in greater length in *ECOpreneuring,* such exchanges are called barter, one of the oldest forms of commercial relationships between people.

The companies or individuals from which you secure your ingredients are also a part of this People equation in marketing. They could likewise share the stage as you craft a story around your products. These vendors, be they farmers or specialty food providers, may also be your biggest cheerleaders as your business dashes from the gate. It's a symbiotic commercial relationship, so they want you to succeed as much as you do and can help share your story, your product and your aspirations. They may also send customers your way. If you are sourcing some of your ingredients from other interesting food artisans, showcase and share their stories on your website.

Partnerships, Networking and Cause-related Marketing

Partnerships can be magnified by cottage food entrepreneurs. While steering away from traditional paid advertising outlets, you may discover strategic partnerships that open new doors to connect with your target audience. When dollars do exchange, like when your business makes a donation or takes out a membership with a non-profit organization, the money goes directly to furthering your shared mission.

Explore ways you can thrive on connections with like-minded organizations. For example, can your bakery products be an add-on to a share for a farm that follows a community supported agriculture (CSA) model? Buy Fresh, Buy Local (foodroutes.org) hosts state and local chapters throughout the country that collaboratively champion locally produced foods.

Or can you join an existing statewide industry association and dovetail your marketing to coincide with their efforts to support artisanal food enterprises? In Wisconsin, we used to have Something Special from Wisconsin, managed through the Wisconsin Department of Agriculture, Trade and Consumer Protection, a state-sponsored marketing program for any business, no matter how small, with at least 50 percent of the product attributable to Wisconsin ingredients, production or processing. The Certified South Carolina (certifiedscgrown.com) program is a cooperative effort among producers, processors, wholesalers, retailers and the South Carolina Department of Agriculture (SCDA) to brand and promote South Carolina products. In Vermont, there's the Vermont Specialty Food Association (vermontspecialty foods.org), among the nation's oldest specialty food associations. See if your state has a similar program.

By joining with non-profit organizations or various causes to help advertise a product, your small enterprise participates in what is commonly called "cause-related marketing." This benefits both the charity or non-profit organization and your business. You cultivate relationships that echo your values, reinforce your business' commitment to the issues you care about and connect with people who share your interests, passions and sense of purpose.

Rather than making donations, with cause-related marketing you create meaningful relationships that help serve the organization with which you partner. This mutually beneficial relationship is particularly salient to a cottage food business, since it offers the ability to co-mingle with much larger organizations that might be trying to improve their brand image and

Beyond the Bottom Line with Hana Lulu's Candy

"Cottage food is really about empowering people to become business owners rather than employees and to develop the confidence to go after their entrepreneurial dreams through baby steps," explains Barbara Preston of San Diego, California. While she sounds like the official spokesperson of her state's home-based food entrepreneur movement, Preston actually sings from the choir. As a self-taught cottage food business owner, she views this legislation as more than a business boost for her Hana Lulu's Candy. "It's all about taking what we know and using that knowledge as a launching pad to help others."

The vision behind Hana Lulu's Candy stems from a vacation Preston took with her husband in Hawaii years ago, driving down a twisty road on Maui and stopping by a roadside stand. "I tasted this candy, a combination of fresh coconut and cane sugar with the crunchy consistency of potato chips, and loved it," Preston describes. "I thought I could order it online when I returned home, but the only thing I found were other people looking for it." This apparent market demand for a unique product led her to try making it herself. After a detailed search online, she found an old recipe. It took another several months of experimentation before she nailed the taste and texture of the candy she had so loved in Hawaii.

While Preston perfected her recipe, her California legislature discussed and passed the *Homemade Food Act* Bill AB 1616, which went into effect on January 1, 2013. "I was one of the first persons to apply for a license in San Diego County," Preston shares. "I learned a lot going through the process and realized other people would be heading down this same road and could learn from my experiences."

This drive to share and collaborate propelled Preston to launch sdcottagefoods.com, where she writes under the pseudonym Cottage Food Sandie. Her site serves as a portal for the movement, offering start-up advice, marketing, pricing and assistance in navigating the regulations.

"Often our cottage food community can share information faster than what comes from the county offices," adds Preston. "For example, we had the applications available online before the county did."

Her collaborative spirit propelled Preston to cross-pollinate her business with supporting a cause close to her heart: The East County Transitional

Name: Barbara Preston

Business: Hana Lulu's Candy (San Diego, California)

Website: hanaluluscandy.com and sdcottagefoods.com

Products: coconut candy

Sales Venue: special order direct to customer; community events, snack stands

Annual Sales: $3,000

Barbara Preston removing tray of her Hana Lulu's coconut candies from her oven. COURTESY OF HANA LULU'S CANDY

Living Center (ECTLC) in El Cajon, a faith-based non-profit supporting men and women battling homelessness. Rather than see her recipe as something exclusively proprietary, she openly taught the women in this program the specific process she developed to make her coconut candy. Preston does have the women sign a confidentiality agreement that they will not disclose or use her recipe in future endeavors. The recipe serves as a stepping stone to help these women garner experience which will help them later in obtaining jobs or starting their own businesses.

"Making candy is a time- and labor-intensive process," Preston recalls. "I saw this as an opportunity for the women at the center to learn empowering skills." As a result, the participants experience teamwork and learn how to run a business, manage inventory and pay bills. With Preston's initiative and support, the women regularly sell at the Scripps Ranch Farmers' Market and earn about a hundred dollars a week. They technically do not operate under the cottage food law because their "home" kitchen is a church kitchen facility, which is not allowed under permitting laws. However, Preston maintains a cottage food license and supports the women in understanding the cottage food business setup so they can readily set up such a business on their own one day.

Close-up of Barbara Preston's coconut candy from Hana Lulu's Candy.
COURTESY OF HANA LULU'S CANDY

In addition to sharing her recipe and business savvy to support the women of ECTLC, Preston also operates Hana Lulu's Candy as her own cottage food venture as a sole proprietor, going to candy-for-community events and on an as-needed basis to fulfill orders. All profits are donated back to the ECTLC. Under California cottage food law, the health department offers two types of permits. The A permit enables operators to sell directly to customers, and the B permit, which Preston holds, allows sales both directly and indirectly to consumers through stores and markets.

Preston sells the small, snack-sized bags for three dollars for one to five bags with discounts for higher quantities, plus delivery charges. "The snack stand at local little league baseball games proved to be a good sales outlet. Parents love a healthier treat option for their kids," she adds.

In California, most cottage food businesses starting out operate as sole proprietors or partnerships because the state requires an eight-hundred-dollar annual fee for corporations. "You really need to get your venture up and running with regular income before investing to take your business structure to the next level," advises Preston.

"Cottage food offers such entrepreneurial potential because it is something you can start while still keeping your full-time day job," sums up Preston. Hana Lulu's Candy offers her an opportunity outside of her corporate career to empower others, as they become food entrepreneurs. "Too often, people feel trapped by this employee mindset that we are all trained for. But cottage food provides the entrepreneurial training wheels to start without taking on big risk." Preston continues to offer advice and insight via her website, particularly encouraging new ventures to tap into some of the ethnic product opportunities on the approved list, like tortillas and fruit-filled tamales.

Always on the lookout for new ways to support others, Preston started mulling a new business vision: "I'd love to someday open a storefront that just sells locally made cottage food products. The range, quality and stories behind our local businesses are incredible. It would be so inspiring to offer all of that in one place."

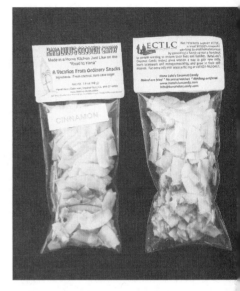

Packaged bags of Hana Lulu's Candy.
COURTESY OF HANA LULU'S CANDY

become more supportive of the local community and the businesses operating there. More and more schools, hospitals and larger corporations are exploring ways to keep their money local. Your cottage food enterprise is a solution to their problem.

Whatever your focus, there's a non-profit group out there with like-minded members. These groups often seek speakers for various events, especially local service organizations like the Kiwanis, Rotary Club and the Optimists. Why not let it be you? As a part of your presentation about your new business, make sure you have plenty of samples — and order forms, too.

Once you're up and running, contributing donations to various non-profit silent auctions can expand your reach to people who might appreciate your generosity to a like-minded cause. People like to buy from people they know, like and respect. Seek out an auction where you can showcase what you make, perhaps in an attractive gift basket. Avoid offering a gift certificate instead of your actual product, since this takes away the eye-candy appeal. If you become over-burdened by donation requests, consider opportunities where you have a visible presence; perhaps you could set up a small sample display during the final night of the auction.

Purpose and Passion

All CFOs work their passion, at least to some extent. You can do what multinational corporations never can to the same degree: communicate honestly, openly and authentically. Everything is personal when you're just starting out. There's no need for customer numbers or a mother's maiden name. You'll be on a first-name basis with your customers. Many are also your friends, neighbors or community members. Instead of a fictional farm representing your strawberry jam, consider putting a picture of the real place on the label.

Purpose-based marketing provides the ultimate in competitive advantage for small businesses; the bigger the operation, the less likely it can maintain its values throughout the company or organization. This is such a challenge for large corporations that whole books are devoted to just this issue. Your sense of purpose and passion can be reflected in everything you do. This compelling message, a part of your inspiring story, puts a face to the food item that your customers then savor, one bite at a time.

By associating your business and product with organizations you support, like the Women's Club, a local entrepreneur group or the chapter of the Sierra Club, you can garner support, build awareness and advocate for issues near and dear to you.

Tips on Nurturing Your Purpose and Passion

These include the following:

Know your elevator pitch

An elevator pitch is a brief "speech" that succinctly describes your cottage food enterprise, something you might say to a stranger chatting with you in an elevator. The most successful CFOs are those who conceived an idea and could express their passion for their product in a way that others could readily understand and support. The elevator pitch is both the "what" you do and the "why."

Maintain your passion

Keeping up your own energy and enthusiasm for your livelihood is important. There will be people who don't care for your product, think you have better things to do with your life or, flat out, don't care that you're happy selling your product and running your own business. Some of the least supportive people might be closest to you, including parents or siblings. Therefore, maintain a network of like-minded people, organizations or businesses to support and encourage you to stay the course and keep at it, even if you accidentally burn a tray of cookies in the oven. It happens to all of us. Find places where you can meet and interact with similarly spirited souls. Such contagious enthusiasm, blended with new insights, often prove to be inspiring.

Manage competition

Unfortunately, you may sense resistance and even be on the receiving end of negative jabs from competing local business owners, especially if they're established enterprises operating in state-licensed commercial kitchens. These businesses may perceive you as competition, which you may or may not be. They may not welcome the fact that you just launched your business from your kitchen with little or no out-of-pocket start-up costs.

Your best play is to keep your head high, remain focused on your customers and ignore the flack. If your product is better than theirs, so be it. In a free market where customers choose the best products at the best prices, that's how it works. In general, competition is a positive force that benefits your community, especially if you account for other aspects of how your business operates, like its impact on the environment or how it builds a stronger local economy. Who knows — you might even improve your competitors' game, too.

Question each other

Like a ping-pong ball, challenging questions should banter back and forth between you and your customers. Ultimately, your business is about serving their needs. Positive in nature, such exchanges stem from the idea that passion should never stagnate. Be open to suggestions, feedback and criticism. That doesn't mean you have to rework your recipes, but one new idea from a customer could lead to a whole new product line that outsells all the others.

Find mentors and *sensei*

In ancient Japanese culture, *sensei* guided the training of ninja and other warriors who practiced the martial arts. In the *Star Wars* world, Jedi Knights are responsible for the training of their Padawan learners. Whenever we step outside our comfort zone and leave behind the safety of routine or seeming normalcy of a "job" with clearly defined responsibilities, we face the unknown. Seek out a mentor or two who possess the sage knowledge and a willingness to serve as a guide, a sounding board or a lifeline as you develop and grow your cottage food enterprise. These mentors can keep you on track, pick you up when you're down and point you in opportunistic directions you never dreamed of.

9

Proving the Market and Getting a Plan

NOW THAT YOU HAVE A HANDLE on your state's cottage food law, set your personal goals for your business, sorted out some possible recipes that might work and embraced the 7 Ps of marketing, it's time to test the market, size up your competition and commit your plan to paper. These final steps are covered in this chapter.

Market Feasibility: Testing the Market

While you may have a great-tasting product, you still have to test it in the marketplace. It's one thing if everyone you know loves your muffins — especially, if they're free. It's something completely different to see if customers will buy them at two dollars a pop. The same holds true for your organic pickles, which you calculated should retail for about twelve dollars a jar.

This process of testing the market for your products is often called a feasibility study; it may take the following route:

(1) **Testing**

This may involve evaluating taste, pricing, portion size, packaging, the label and even the sales venue itself.

(2) **Feedback**

Provide comment cards, send short online product surveys, or have a system in place where you can jot down or collect comments you receive from customers about your product. While some feedback may echo what your customers think you want to hear (not what you really want), other times it could highlight an issue, sometimes in a brutally honest way.

Besides reaching out directly for feedback, you can also explore incidental sources of information about your most promising markets. How are other food enterprises selling their products? Having some competition is a great thing, since that means there's a market for what you want to sell. Evaluate each of the 7 Ps of marketing in relation to your competitors to determine how your products are different — and better.

(3) Refinement

Take what you've learned, by way of direct customer feedback or observing decisions made by your customers or the marketplace, and refine, modify or adjust your product and marketing accordingly. For example, did your blueberry muffins sell out in the first hour, but you returned home with your wild cherry version? Did a volume discount pricing strategy for your gift jellies allow you to profit more by selling a greater volume than if you sold them all one at a time at full price? Did a flavor sampler set sell better than a four-pack of the same flavor?

Keep refining until you've reached a level of confidence before launching your product. Remember, you need to have a product that enough customers want and are willing to pay for at a fair price, to leave you with enough profit at the end of the day to make it worth undertaking.

(4) Product Launch

Finally, synthesize your testing, feedback and refinement into your final product and implement your launch campaign.

Keep in mind, however, that change is constant. Customers can be fickle, follow trends and fads, or have tastes that change. One year, gluten-free is the rage; three years later, it's sugar-free or low-sugar. In most cases, even though your feasibility study may reveal solid products to market, it's always possible that market conditions will change, a new competitor will show up across from your booth or some of your key customers will move away.

The food industry, especially specialty food products, can be cyclical and very sensitive to economic booms and busts. By their nature, many of these

Fermenting Dough with Home-Baked Bread

"I'm a small-scale nano-farmer looking to keep the income going in the winter," shares Regina Dlugokencky, owner of Seedsower Farm, a little market farm operation in Long Island, New York. What started as an after-thought to the farming season fermented into a bread-making obsession for this self-taught baker. "You could say I've built a nice little cult follow-ing for my bread," she adds. "I'm now known as 'the organic bread girl' at our farmers' market."

Dlugokencky sells sourdough breads along with organic jams every Sunday from December though April at the Long Island Winter Farmers' Market in Huntington Station, New York. Using only organic ingredients and New York State flours, she quickly discovered the sweet spot in starting a bread business: all you need is flour and yeast, and, with a fresh product like bread, you can start super-small and test market demand for different products and adapt as you move along.

"The first time I experimented with bread at the market, I just brought six loaves. I used one for sampling and quickly sold the other five. I was hooked on the potential." Like many cottage food operators, Dlugokencky used the farmers' markets as "test markets" for her products, examining customer preferences and sensitivity to price and gauging demand.

Today she bakes thirty to forty loaves each week. The loaves sell for between $5.00 and $6.50 each. In the spring, Dlugokencky also raises organic vegetable garden plants. Her other growing season focus is raising crops that will serve as additional products for the winter markets, such as berries for her jams and storable alliums like garlic, shallots

Name: Regina Dlugokencky

Business: Seedsower Farm (Centerport, New York)

Website: seedsowerfarm.com

Products: sourdough bread, jam, sourdough popovers, focaccia

Sales venue: farmers' market

Annual Sales: $3,000

Seedsower Farm owner Regina Dlugokencky holding her fresh-baked bread. COURTESY OF SEEDSOWER FARM

Seedsower Farm's artisanal breads, ready for packing for market.
<small>COURTESY OF SEEDSOWER FARM</small>

and specialty onions. She cures these to sell at the winter markets.

Blending efficiency and a dedication to frugality, Dlugokencky creates various systems and organizational techniques to turn out loaves from her small kitchen. "I didn't go out and buy everything right away when I started. Instead, I tapped into friends' offers to help. It amazed me how many folks owned multiple KitchenAid mixers and were happy to let me borrow theirs." The morning before market, she makes the dough, using a sourdough starter instead of yeast, which gives the bread that desirable tangy taste and crusty texture. She lets the KitchenAid mixer do the heavy work of kneading. The dough is then placed in large containers for the long, first rise.

After an initial rise of three to four hours, she divides the dough and weighs each piece on a scale for consistent loaf size, finding that her customers generally like a smaller loaf (weighing about a pound after baking). After a short rest time, she shapes the loaves and places the divided dough in various bowls, covers them with plastic wrap, and places them in the refrigerator for the final, slow rise overnight. "When I first began baking, the bowls were nothing special, just what I already had on hand," she says. But once she found the market for her bread was viable, she invested in proofing baskets. "I want to keep the product accessible to the most number of people, so I place my investment in the ingredients and try to be resourceful with everything else."

At 2 am the next morning, Dlugokencky's morning baking is in full swing. She preheats the oven and removes the loaves from the refrigerator, where they've been since the day before, to come back to room temperature. To make a 10 am market start, she then bakes from 3:00 to 8:30 am.

"I highly recommend using proofing baskets instead of bowls for the final rise. The baskets will make your loaf look phenomenal, like it came out of a professional bakery," advises Dlugokencky. Proofing baskets, also called *bannetons*, come in every shape and size — round, oval or long. Sprinkle the basket generously with flour and place the dough inside for the final rise. The lines and pattern of the basket will imprint on your dough in a beautiful pattern. Flip the dough out after it has risen and you're ready to bake.

"My biggest challenge is baking all the bread in my kitchen in time for market. I killed my first oven three times, perhaps due to volume, and finally invested in a large 5.6-cubic-feet oven with convection. Now I can bake eight loaves at a time." She thoroughly researched models and corresponding reviews before deciding on a Kenmore that met her $1,000 budget. "I actually considered buying a commercial oven, but the electricity would have to be redone, and, technically, a home processor's license in New York disallows use of professional equipment."

"At market, let your customers pick out which loaf they like," Dlugokencky suggests. "It's an easy way to add that personal touch and interact with them." She also makes a few batches of onion focaccia and sourdough popovers, which she sells individually. These add a tempting impulse purchase since they're something her customers can eat right away while taking the loaf of bread home.

"I prepare jams from the summer berry harvest, but I confess I like making bread better. The jam is a much smaller side business of less than 20 percent of my total sales," adds Dlugokencky. In addition to the berries she grows herself, she buys local, organic fruit in bulk in season and freezes it to make jams during the winter. She does charge a $1.50 deposit for the jar to keep the costs down and finds customers have no issue with that, even though she rarely gets the jar back. As a vendor at the Long Island Farmers' Market, Dlugokencky must carry both general and product liability insurance which she gets through Farm Family Insurance for a couple hundred dollars a year.

There's nothing like Seedsower Farm's jam to go with fresh-baked bread.
COURTESY OF SEEDSOWER FARM

"Start small and keep learning," Dlugokencky advises. "Once you find out what you like to do, like me with bread, fine-tune your recipes and don't be afraid to fail. The first loaf of bread I made doesn't compare to what I can pump out in multiple batches every week now. It took practice and some mess-ups along the way."

The focaccia baked by Regina Dlugokencky gives her customers a chance to snack while at the market. COURTESY OF SEEDSOWER FARM

Dlugokencky's frugal nature embraces and celebrates the failures: any bread not fit for eating makes great breadcrumbs or croutons!

food items are perceived as impulse purchases. A breakfast of chocolate croissants is not the same thing as a hearty spaghetti dinner in the eyes of many, even if both cost about the same.

Be realistic, flexible and adaptable with your products and marketing and you'll do just fine. And keep listening to the needs of your customers. They might just point you in the direction of the next great thing.

Competitive Analysis

Early on in your product development, you'll need to undertake some form of competitive analysis, carefully examining the potential markets for your products. This will give you a sense of what other companies are selling and

Garnering Feedback

As a small CFO, you don't need to spin wheels and spend lots of money to figure out the value and sales viability of your product. Depending on your products, options to connect with your customers and garner actionable information may include:

- Follow-up e-mails requesting customer comments or feedback.

- Testing out products at mini-markets. By selling at small sales venues to test the waters with your product, you can adjust various marketing approaches, including price, to determine the potential for your product.

- Snail mail a letter with a small survey to return in a self-addressed stamped envelope.

- Try out the widely used Survey Monkey (surveymonkey.com), a free online system that allows you to invite customers to complete a survey about your products; SurveyMonkey provides various analytic tools to ferret out key insights.

- Large marketing companies often use focus groups, inviting potential customers to taste samples and offer their opinions. You could do something similar, perhaps in a less formal way at your home or a "community room" at your local library, if they permit it.

Regardless of how you collect feedback, make sure you incentivize your customers' participation. As thanks, perhaps offer a giveaway draw for your products. In your early market feasibility study, you may want to avoid social media until you're satisfied with your products and feel comfortable that the public feedback you receive will generally be favorable. Ideally, minimize the possibility of customers railing or venting negatively about your product, especially if you're still refining your recipe or the marketing. If you've ever read restaurant reviews on Yelp or Trip Advisor, you'll recognize the power of one that's well written but scathing.

how their products are the same as or similar to what you want to offer. Observe pricing, product features and other marketing aspects.

Competitive analysis can be informal, via the Internet, or merely anecdotal, perhaps as you browse the aisles of a local farmers' market or arts and craft show, jotting down notes on the selection, pricing and quality of baked goods. An easy way to record your findings is by creating a chart or matrix that lists other companies and their products, along with any distinguishing characteristics or special features.

Many enterprises come about because a particular food product is completely missing where they're located. Perhaps there are no organic pickles, gluten-free baked goods or decorative cakes made in a nut-free kitchen. In these cases, you'll have the opportunity to "own the market" and be the only one offering such an item. But be warned: this doesn't guarantee success or mean you can charge anything you want. You'll still need enough customers in your community who want to buy your product at a fair price to make your enterprise worth undertaking.

The more ambitious your plans and sales goals, the more astute you'll need to be to details, competition and marketing considerations. Understanding your competition is essential to breaking into the market with your products. The more crowded a market, the more you'll need to find your niche and clearly identify your target audience, both covered previously in Chapter 4.

Planning for Profits

Finally, the time has come to put it all together. If you've followed along in the previous chapters, making notes, testing recipes, coming up with product names, talking with potential customers, and making labels, it's time to summarize everything in a plan and then put that plan into action.

The Back-of-the-napkin Plan

If you fail to plan, you plan to fail. Some of the most innovative ideas or tastiest recipes never make it to our mouths because the people with them couldn't get their ideas down on the drawing table or, worse yet, jumped into a business before thinking it all the way through. Please don't let this happen to you.

Given that most cottage food businesses will have modest or humble beginnings, we're recommending that you forget about writing a full-blown business plan with a vision statement, company description, product details, strategy...ad nauseum. At this point, you don't need to impress a bank to get a loan to start your business. It's too early to tell if your cookies are going to be a ten-thousand or a hundred-thousand-dollar hit.

That said, if you love writing or like to meticulously detail every step, decision and ingredient, by all means do so, but know that such a labor-intensive undertaking is unlikely to make your business more profitable when you're just starting out. It's the process of writing the business plan that's most valuable. It forces you to evaluate every aspect of your enterprise and get these details down on paper.

If the time comes where you need and want to expand, you'll have plenty of time, enthusiasm and determination then to pull together that business plan that would impress an MBA professor type, lure money from the deep pockets of bankers and convince the rest of your family you're serious about turning your cottage food business into a big business, covered in the last section of this book. There are plenty of free online resources that guide you through the steps of writing a business plan, from a vision statement to pro forma income statement and balance sheet. In case you're curious, here are a few that you can customize for your needs: enloop.com, score.org; sba.gov (follow the link to writing a business plan).

Besides providing resources for small businesses, the Association for America's Small Business Development Centers (asbdc-us.org) offers a small business assistance network in the United States and its territories. The network's mission is to help new entrepreneurs realize their dreams of business ownership. Small business owners and aspiring entrepreneurs can go to one of approximately a thousand local SBDCs for free, face-to-face business consulting and at-cost training on writing business plans, marketing or regulatory compliance. For the non-profit Business Alliance for Local Living Economies (BALLE), it's all about being a "localist." Their mantra: "Changing the way our economy operates starts with a single person. It starts with you. We believe that real national prosperity begins at the local level." BALLE recognizes that local independently owned businesses are the key to solving communities' toughest challenges and to creating real prosperity. BALLE (bealocalist.org) connects visionary local leaders so they can find inspiration and support; they're another place to go to expand your market for cottage foods and network with others with similar interests.

But for now, let's go with what we call the "back-of-a-napkin plan" that, if nothing else, makes sure you don't forget the great ideas you've come up with to get your product to market. Plus, it might keep you on track. As an example, the adjacent sidebar provides a sample napkin-sized plan for our Inn Serendipity FRESH BAKED business, specific to our state's pending cottage food law; a general template is on this book's website.

When searching for resources to help you launch your business, you'll sometimes notice a bias against being your own boss or becoming an entrepreneur, especially at universities where tenure is still practiced. Our mantra: give your business idea a shot, get a plan together and go for it. So,

Inn Serendipity FRESH BAKED

Products: Biscotti, granola, organic muffins, bagels, granola bars

Sales Objective: $2,000, ramping up to Wisconsin's cap of $10,000 gross sales

Target Markets:
- Primary: Inn Serendipity Bed & Breakfast guests; direct on-farm sales
- Secondary: Attendees at various community events; direct-to-customer sales at a booth

Niche: Baked products made with organic and locally sourced ingredients, containing no artificial flavors, colors or preservatives

Positioning Statement: Inn Serendipity FRESH BAKED offers discriminating foodies great-tasting, truly homemade, organic and locally baked goods that contain no artificial flavors, colors or preservatives. These premium-priced products are unlike any available in the Monroe, Wisconsin, area.

Sales Venues: On-site, plus some high-traffic, low-competition community events during the low season, like Monroe Cheese Days and Monroe Gem and Rock Show

Start-up expenses: $25 total, for cottage food license ($10) and required online food safety training course ($15). The equipment and business registrations (sales tax = $10); state license ($65) and registered office registration ($25), are already covered as a part of Inn Serendipity B&B.

Fixed expenses: $0, liability insurance covered by existing homeowner policy from Cincinnati Insurance Company as a part of the B&B; the B&B is listed as "incidental to the home" and comes with an annual premium of $69. Additionally, $1 million umbrella liability insurance policy is also taken, costing $165 per year. DSL Internet service ($34/month), domain name ($10/year) and website hosting ($120/year) already covered as a part of the business.

take any negative vibes you might encounter in stride and recognize the source. It could be coming from an ivory tower.

Here's how one less-than-positive start-up guide written by Kenneth W. Wood from the Mississippi State University Extension Service puts it:

> *"Do I want a hobby, or do I want to make money?" It is very difficult to introduce a new product into the market place. In many instances, it would be better to take the money required to start such a business and invest it in a certificate of deposit.*

Oh, really? Last we checked, you can earn only .99% APY on a CD for one year; for a $500 investment, you'd get back $4.95 in interest earnings. We don't know a cottage food business on the planet that couldn't beat that.

Don't let anyone discourage your enthusiasm for making some dough — both figuratively and literally — with fresh baked dinner rolls.
JOHN D. IVANKO

Organizing, Planning and Managing the Business

SECTION 3

10

Ready, Set, Go: Organize Your Kitchen

I F YOU'RE LIKE MOST FOLKS starting a cottage food business, you already know your way around a kitchen. It may very well be your favorite spot in the house, where you bake up your holiday cookie favorites or Sunday morning muffins.

The key next step, and what this chapter covers, is how to shift from being a homespun casual cook to viewing your kitchen as the base for a viable business enterprise. It's like your kitchen now has dual personalities. On one side, it's still the hub of your family meals and routines. On the flip side, it transforms into an efficient production facility where you pump out your pickles and pound cake like nobody's business.

Take your kitchen setup seriously and make the time to organize systems that ensure food safety. By keeping things under control and practicing proper procedures, you avoid stress, inefficiency and food safety issues. This chapter will offer suggestions on how to do just that.

Five Steps for Setting Up Your Home Processing Facility

By now you figured out your recipe and developed your product and the marketing that goes with it. Next, set up your kitchen so you can make ten dozen brownies as easily as one dozen. If you're operating out of a tiny apartment or urban kitchen, this will take especially careful planning. Since you can feed your extended family a Thanksgiving turkey dinner, you can pull off making cases of strawberry-rhubarb jam, too.

As much as you can, separate personal use from business use; in some states, this is required by law. There will be overlap in your kitchen, particularly as it relates to use of space, from counters to mixers. The magic of a cottage food business is that you don't need to buy a lot of new equipment.

However, items that are clearly business-only, such as product ingredients, need to be stored, labeled clearly and tracked separately.

Step 1: Assess Equipment

What recipes are you making? What equipment do you need to make it? Write out a list answering both these questions. The list will vary depending on the type of food product you make; typical answers for baked products and canned items are covered below.

For baked products:

The KitchenAid stand mixer is a go-to appliance for author Lisa Kivirist in her home kitchen at Inn Serendipity.

JOHN D. IVANKO

- **Stand mixer**

  A stand mixer will be much more efficient than a hand mixer when it comes to preparing batters and dough. A stand mixer frees up your hands for other tasks, and, with its mighty motor, the batter at the end will have a smoother texture and bake more evenly. Most models come with a wire beater attachment that adds air as it turns to keep batter light and fluffy. A stand mixer, a heavy and clunky piece of equipment, requires more storage space; they're not cheap either. The difference between various models comes down to how they handle dense dough; the more solid — and pricier — models tend to do this better.

  Stand mixers come with different bowl sizes, ranging from three- to seven-quart. If you're in the market to purchase a new mixer, bigger will always be better and more efficient for mixing multiple batches. If you have the funds for a larger mixer up to the seven-quart size, give it serious consideration. Having extra mixing bowls helps, allowing you to prep one bowl while another is mixing, and extra small bowls mean less washing if you're only beating something small. Double-check that any extra bowls you order work with your make and model of stand mixer. KitchenAid (kitchenaid.com) mixer accessories have a reputation for being interchangeable.

  Another stand mixer add-on particularly helpful to cottage food baking enterprises is a pouring shield, a plastic edge that sits on top of your mixing bowl and keeps ingredients, particularly light stuff like flour, inside the bowl where they belong. A range of other add-on attachments use the stand mixer motor and transform it into another appliance, from a food processor to a pasta roller.

- **Hand mixer**

A hand mixer is much lighter in weight and better for small, simple tasks, like whipping one egg white. Because a hand mixer has less power than a stand mixer, avoid over-tasking it with denser dough or batter; otherwise, you'll burn out the motor. Oster (oster.com) makes a rechargeable, cordless hand mixer that's versatile and easy to store.

- **Baking pans**

Multiple baking pans help you operate efficiently by maximizing baking time. While one set of cookies bake, you can prep another and keep rotating. Most home ovens have three racks that can accommodate three cookie sheets, so having six cookie sheets will triple your output in half the time. Buying identical pans helps with storage since they fit on top of each other easily.

The most versatile pan in your baking setup will probably be the sheet pan, also called a cookie sheet. You'll be using this pan so much that it's worth the time to research one that will hold up to hundreds of uses. Cookie sheets come in various materials, sizes, thicknesses and finishes, insulated or not, with rims or not. To bake items evenly without burning, thicker sheets work best and are less likely to warp over time than thinner or insulated sheets. Sheets with rims tend to be easier to handle, and the sides prevent anything from running over and spilling in your oven. Of course, get as big a sheet as will fit in your oven to maximize baking space.

Some new products make baking easier. The COOKINA Cuisine Reusable Cooking Sheet (cookina.co) from Poirier Richard Inc. creates a non-stick, easy-to-clean alternative to aluminum foil, parchment or wax paper. Place it on your sheet pan or baking tray to bake without oil. The sheet is easy to clean with soap and water afterwards and does not hold

COOKINA Cuisine Reusable Cooking Sheet holding two croissants, easily lifted off the non-stick surface.
COURTESY OF COOKINA/POIRIER RICHARD INC.

odors or flavors from previous uses. It is 100 percent non-stick and PFOA-free, reusable and reversible. The company also makes a COOKINA Gard Oven Protector to catch spills and a COOKINA Grilling Sheet for barbecue grilling.

Another route to go is food-grade silicon bread or pastry liners and flexible molds from Sasa Demarle (sasademarle.com). They have a Silpat Workstation Roul'pat (silpat.com) that is coated with silicon on both sides, allowing you to roll out any kind of dough without using flour; it also allows for spreading nougat, cooked sugar, chocolate or caramel. Their molds come in various shapes and sizes for pastries, specialty breads and muffins, but you'll need to go to a restaurant supply store for these. Their Silpain non-stick baking mat for breads has perforated qualities. The water seeps through the mat, leaving a crusty finish for your homemade biscuits and breads.

- **Cooling racks**
  Don't just let your baked items cool in the pan. Cooling racks are essential for the baking process. Unlike trivets or hot pads, they allow air to circulate underneath the rack, so the item in your baking pan cools down faster and doesn't over-bake or dry out.

  Cooling racks can take up a lot of valuable counter space, so look for a stacked rack that uses your existing cookie sheets and lets you stack four, one above the other, with plenty of air space for circulation in between each. King Arthur Flour (kingarthurflour.com) makes a stacked rack that holds four sheets and folds down for easy storage.

For Canning:

Even if you're already a home canner, when you're making cases of products, you'll want to have the following canning items on hand.

- **Water bath canner and rack or pressure canner**
  If you've been getting by with a stock pot and a MacGyvered rack out of rolled foil, let your business launch be the reason to upgrade to an official water bath canner with a fitted metal rack. Designed to fit perfectly into your water bath canner, these sturdy racks are easy to lift out and allow you to both put in and take out a full batch of jars all at once.

What Is Food-Grade Plastic?

Not all plastic is suitable for food storage or for using in the food preparation process. The US Food and Drug Administration (FDA) requires that plastics that come into contact with food are of a higher purity and not harmful to humans. If you're looking for storage buckets and bins — or a plastic container for proofing your bread dough — below are a few considerations.

- **Use recycled containers previously used for food.**
  Restaurants and other food service establishments can be good resources for free, large, food-grade containers, such as five-gallon buckets that were once filled with potato salad or soy sauce. Of course, you'll need to clean and sanitize them thoroughly before use.

- **Look for food safe symbols.**
  A cup and fork is the universal symbol for food-safe plastic.

- **Identify HDPE: Number 2 plastic.**
  The plastic recycling number "2" indicates "high-density polyethylene" (HDPE), one of the most inert and stable forms of plastic. All plastic food-grade buckets used at restaurants will be made from HDPE. Not all HDPE plastic is safe, however. Look for the stamped markings FDA, NSF or the cup and fork symbol to confirm the plastic is food-safe HDPE.

- **Buy from a kitchen retailer.**
  Purchasing items specifically designed for the kitchen, such as food storage containers from the Container Store or Bed, Bath & Beyond, will ensure food-grade plastic is used. Restaurant supply stores that service caterers will have larger, more functional plastic food-service containers that are often cheaper than those available at chain retailers.

Pressure canners went through a major redesign in the 1970s, resulting in today's modern design that's much safer due to improved gauges for regulating pressure. While pressure canners are an approved method for sealing jars, they involve more steps and detail than water bath canners. The National Center of Home Preservation (nchfp.uga.edu/) has specific resources for the step-by-step process of safe pressure canning.

- **Wide-mouth funnel**
Keeps your product in your jar and off your counter. Norpro (norpro.com) makes a stainless-steel version.

Canning in a home kitchen requires attention to the recipe and the process, but it's not hard if you have the right tools.
JOHN D. IVANKO

- **Jar lifter**

  Works better and safer than kitchen tongs to help move hot jars for the water bath.

- **Lid wand**

  Enables you to remove sanitized jar lids from the boiling water without burning your fingers or contaminating the lid.

- **Large cleaning brush**

  Helps scrub out any debris as you prepare your jars. Typically made from a sponge material adhered to a handle.

General Equipment

In addition to the key baking or canning equipment, think through the following equipment for your cottage food operation that, while shared with other people in your home, is still essential for your enterprise.

- **Refrigerator**

  You already have a refrigerator — now you need to sort out how to handle the increased storage needs your enterprise will bring. Be sure to cover, date and label all ingredients used in your items. Go for square food storage containers since they use space more efficiently than round ones. Required by many cottage food regulations, place a thermometer designed for refrigerators in the back of your unit and make sure your unit maintains a temperature between 38 and 44 degrees Fahrenheit (3 to 7 degrees Celsius).

  Depending on what you're making and your available space, you may need a second refrigerator. This second unit, used exclusively for the business, could be a capital business expense. It will both give you extra space and avoid confusion with your home items and what the kids know they can snack on. A second refrigerator will also minimize food odor issues, which could jeopardize the taste of your products. Home refrigerators may hold a range of items and the smells they bring with them, like a spicy curry, garlicky potatoes or a fish dish. A second refrigerator stops such smells influencing the flavor of your dough or frosted cake.

- **Food processor**

  A real ninja in the kitchen: the food processor. It can slice, dice, chop and puree, making a variety of prep tasks more efficient. Get a food processor

Kitchen Considerations: Ovens and Cooktops

Before visions of a cottage food business danced in your head, your oven and cooktop probably served as the workhorses of your home kitchen. Whether you own a dual element with an oven built in underneath the cooktop or two separate units, you probably use them every day, for everything from baking birthday cakes to simmering soups. But now that you've stepped up production in your home kitchen, make sure these two pieces of equipment can handle the new workload. Do your research to ensure you invest in what's best for your needs.

Options and considerations vary, depending on if you use gas or electricity to power these two large appliances. For cooking, professional chefs and home foodies tend to be loyal to gas since you can better control the heat and the gas burners; both heat up and cool down fast. But electric appliances come with built-in safety features, because they don't have pilot lights that can go out and cause gas leaks. Electric cooktops come with different burner sizes to heat pots or pans efficiently. Flat-top electric cook surfaces are also easy to clean.

The other kitchen contemplation involves potentially investing in a commercial-grade oven or cooktop, akin to what you'd find in the kitchen of a restaurant. Some variables to think about when researching commercial equipment:

- **Determine space and setup requirements**
  Often double the size of a standard home unit, commercial appliances generally require more floor space. Additionally, because a commercial oven generates high heat, such a unit needs to be at least six inches away from the wall and may also require the wall to be tiled or covered in metal to protect it from this heat. Commercial units may also require more complicated, and therefore expensive, ventilation. Be sure your house can handle the gas or electric needs of such commercial units. Remember, most ranges use gas.

- **Research heat output and insulation**
  Generally, home units are much better insulated than commercial-grade units, meaning the commercial versions will let off more heat into your home and often be hot to the touch. A commercial oven might then cause you to run — and pay for — more air-conditioning in the summer if you operate a baking business. Do you have young kids in the kitchen at times you're not baking for the businesses — little hands that might touch the unit and burn themselves? Alternatives include commercial models specifically designed for the home. Higher-end appliance companies like Viking and Wolf offer such units that, while pricey (they run into the thousands of dollars), provide commercial quality and function but are well-insulated and designed for a home kitchen layout.

- **Check insurance requirements**
  Because of the high-heat nature of commercial equipment, your insurance policy may not allow such an oven or cooktop under your standard homeowner's policy. ☛

Another home cooktop option to consider is induction. Induction instantly heats up a pan by using an electromagnetic field. This leaves the cooking surface cool to the touch as soon as the pan is removed and does not heat the air around the cooktop. While safer and more energy-efficient than either gas or electric, induction cooktops come at a higher price tag of more than a thousand dollars; they also require all pots and pans to be made out of something with iron, like steel or cast iron, which may require an additional investment.

with a large cup size for large batch processing; Cuisinart (cuisinart.com) has bowl sizes that range from seven- to fourteen-cup. Food processors often come with a wide open tube at the top called a "feed tube" that allows you to push larger pieces in at one time. Look for a model designed for effective storage with retractable cords and specific compartments to store attachments like blades.

- **Timer**
Don't lose track of time when you have multiple recipes baking, proofing and mixing. Most smartphones come with timers. The good old wind-up versions are great standbys and can be carried around with you to different rooms. Avoid over-using the oven or microwave timers, prematurely frying the electrical motherboard and losing your oven controls in the process.

Step 2: Inventory Ingredients

Since you're doing larger batches than you typically would for home use, you'll need to take managing your ingredients up a notch. "Make do" or substitutes in a recipe are out. Having everything on hand before you start is essential.

To get a handle on your ingredients, list everything you need for your recipes and their approximate quantities. As you scale up in quantity, consider converting your recipes to weight measurements. Changing "cups" to "ounces and pounds" makes calculating total amounts easier. Use a calibrated scale for weighing quantities.

Should you purchase larger quantities in a bulk bag, you'll need your own storage containers and a system to keep track of your ingredients and make sure they're fresh. Heavy-duty, food-grade plastic bins can be found at the Container Store and restaurant supply stores. This one-time investment ensures that your ingredients remain fresh and safe while in storage.

Whether your ingredients are refrigerated, like milk or butter, or stored in the pantry, like chocolate chips, use the "first food in, first food out" inventory principle; use the oldest ingredient first to keep inventory fresh. If an item doesn't have an easy-to-read expiration or "purchase by" date, write the date you purchased it directly on the package with a Sharpie permanent marker. Make sure everything is sealed and covered when stored. If you store items in glass jars, mark dates on the glass with the Sharpie. When the jars are empty, use rubbing alcohol to remove the permanent marker notations. Adhesive stickers can work, too, but they're more likely to fall off or get stained when wet; plus the labels leave glue residue on the jar when it comes time to remove them.

Some cottage food laws require that ingredients you use for your business be separated somehow from those used in your home for personal consumption. For refrigerated items, CFOs often dedicate a shelf to work ingredients. For dry ingredients, bins, cabinet shelves and racks may be set aside for business-use-only ingredients.

Step 3: Organize the Kitchen

Now that you have a handle on your equipment and ingredients, how will you use your kitchen space most effectively to access and use these items when you're in production flow? Organization improves your operation on many levels: efficiency; cleanliness; ease of use; food safety. Take the following actions to organize and streamline your production.

- **Clear clutter**
  You can never have enough workspace, so move out anything non-essential, especially anything decorative. Create as large and clear a workspace as you can. Potted plants, antiques, collectibles and that random cookie

jar need to go. Kitchen space may be limited, so pack up seasonal items like the Thanksgiving turkey roaster or summertime ice pop molds and store them far away. You probably have some dishes taking space in your cabinets that are only used intermittently or for larger dinner parties. Again, find space somewhere else.

- **Designate cabinets specifically for business inventory**
  This separation gives clear distinction between your personal kitchen and cottage food business and may enable you to calculate and manage your expenses more clearly. If you just dip into your home inventory for ingredients, how will you figure out how much money you are making? Focus on high-volume dry goods that you use for your business, like flour and sugar for baking, and keep those separate. That teaspoon of salt or cinnamon might not matter so much to your bottom line, but some ingredients, like vanilla extract and saffron, are expensive. If your recipes regularly call for high-cost ingredients, keep a separate set of these for business use only. Always keep cleaning supplies stored separately and away from food products.

- **Add storage space**
  Any under-utilized spots in your kitchen? Can you add shelves? Chrome wire shelving racks can hold up to 500 pounds. Mount some sturdy stainless steel S hooks on them to hang your large pots or bulky utensils. Likewise, add hooks to the inside of your pantry door to hang lighter items like kitchen towels or a strainer.

  Keep your key supplies where you can access them readily and you'll reduce your preparation time. Consider adding a lazy Susan spinning turntable inside cabinets that holds items like spices and flavorings for easy access. If your cabinet runs deep, consider adding pull-out shelving so you don't always have to reach into the back and fumble around looking for items.

  Don't forget, you may need storage space for your final product, depending on what it is. Canned items are easiest since they're shelf-stable and can go anywhere in the house that is cool and dark, like on basement shelving. Most baked goods not yet packaged can go in large food-grade containers, then be stacked. Items made close to the time of sale can be placed directly from the cooling rack to bakery boxes or bags for transport.

Step 4: Manage Time

Managing your time is integral to your cottage food business mix. To reduce stress, increase enjoyment and ensure profits, keep the following considerations in mind.

- **Plan your schedule**

  How and when you work in the kitchen will depend on what you're making. Canned items like jams and jellies can be made weeks before a sale. Your production schedule for those items will be based around when the ingredients are available. If you're making strawberry jam from your bountiful garden patch, you'll need to reserve time blocks for major canning sessions during that peak June harvest. You can then label at your leisure and sell year-round.

  For baked and other fresh goods, your production timing needs to be closer to the actual sale. If you're making one key item, like a large order of cinnamon rolls for a breakfast meeting at an office, you can get everything organized the night before, bake the rolls that morning and you're done. However, if you're preparing for a farmers' market or festival booth where you envision selling a range of baked items, plan your production schedule accordingly. See if there are some items, like cookies, that can be made a day or two in advance so you can free up the day before for the items that need to be super fresh, like bread or muffins.

- **Establish family boundaries**

  While cottage food laws open up a wealth of stay-at-home business opportunities, integrating a business into established home routines isn't always easy, especially if everyone in the family is used to 24/7 kitchen access and snacks on demand.

  Carve out specific time blocks for your business kitchen work. While an older child may be capable of offering assistance, younger children likely to stick fingers in batter should be kept out of the kitchen when you're filling an order. Rearrange your refrigerator magnet collection and post your production schedule for the week for all to see. When planning

Parbaking

Consider "parbaking" when planning your baking schedule, especially at a time when you need a lot of fresh items finished simultaneously for a market or event. Parbaking means baking bread or other dough-based items partially and then freezing them and finishing the baking at a later time. For bread, this initial baking phase both kills the yeast and cooks up the inside of the loaf, forming the internal structure of the proteins and starches that gives the loaf its spongy internal texture.

After this initial bake, cool and freeze the item. When you're ready for the final loaf, bake it a bit more to form the crust. This saves time during your final baking rush and typically won't diminish the taste or texture of your product.

Experiment with a few batches to determine exactly what parbaking procedures work for your specific recipe.

Generally cut about 25 percent off your full cook time for the initial bake; for example, if your bread cooks for an hour, parbake it at the same temperature for 45 minutes. With parbaking, you want to bake the bread long enough to get it to an internal temperature of about 185 °F (85 °C) for softer crusts such as sandwich loaves and at least 205 °F (96 °C) for harder, more rustic crusts.

Once the item cools after the initial bake, let it fully cool to room temperature. Give it time as this can take up to two hours for a dense loaf of bread. Once completely cooled, tightly wrap the item in plastic wrap like Saran Wrap, add another layer of tightly wrapped foil for added preservation and freeze.

Right before you need your final product, take the loaf out of the freezer and place it in an oven preheated to your regular baking temperature; bake it that remaining 25 percent of your full baking time, typically ten to fifteen minutes or until golden brown.

your day, avoid letting your business take over your life. Of course, you want to care for your customers. But this shouldn't come at the expense of your family or personal well-being.

- **Take physical care**
Standing on your feet for hours in the kitchen can quickly add up; you'll feel it in your bones. Remember that by caring for yourself, you're boosting your business success in the long run. Keep changing positions. Sit down and do certain activities at a tabletop as much as possible, like decorating cookies. Take stretch breaks and do a few yoga moves to get the

blood flowing in between tasks. Get outside for some fresh air, perhaps with a walk around the block or meander through your garden.

Consider investing in a gel mat, a heavy-duty floor mat made from polyurethane that cushions the hard floor and makes things easier on your joints when standing for long-periods of time. GelPro (gelpro.com) and Imprint (imprintmats.com) both make such mats that retail in the fifty to one-hundred dollar range. They're well worth the investment if you are standing in one place at the counter for hours on end — you won't feel it nearly as much in your legs at the end of the day.

Before starting a kitchen processing session, feed yourself first. Make sure you eat a healthy meal and drink plenty of water. It's easy to forget this step and later find yourself "testing" or snacking on those batches of shortbread as they come out of the oven. You want your muffin business to bring in cash, not add a muffin top!

Keep the cooking process fun. Play some music to sustain your energy. Try listing to podcasts or books on tape to make the processing time more interesting and less tedious. At times, you may find yourself feeling lonely or isolated as a one-person operation. Besides inviting "helpers" to participate, consider donning a headset phone and chatting with friends or family, if it's not too distracting from the business at hand.

Step 5: Practice Proper Food Safety

Proper food safety procedures form the foundation of your business, ensuring the quality and safety of your product. Make our cottage food industry proud by proving that a fully licensed commercial kitchen isn't a synonym for food safety; home-based operations can be as safe, if not safer. You wouldn't poison your own family, so why would feeding the public be any different? Remember you are cooking for the public and look at your kitchen from the eyes of a potential customer; make sure it sparkles and confidently communicates cleanliness so that anyone would feel safe eating what is prepared there. Making something in your home kitchen and sharing it exemplifies the ultimate in trust. Celebrate that fact by prioritizing safe procedures in your kitchen every day.

Having reviewed your state cottage food law, you'll have noticed the requirements related to sanitation and food safety. It may be as simple as reading and practicing a basic checklist of proper procedures. Or there may

be a specific requirement list and a mandatory on-site inspection. Don't panic if your kitchen will be inspected; just make sure it is spotless and double-check any list of requirements. The morning of the inspection is not the time to do anything unusual, like unplugging the refrigerator to clean behind it. What if your refrigerator doesn't readily start back up again or the temperature isn't at the "safe" level on the thermometer? Don't jeopardize your inspection. Have everything ready and operational the day before and avoid the stress.

Many states require some form of "certified food handler" license, similar to what employees in restaurants would have. ServSafe, operated through the National Restaurant Association (servsafe.com), offers an annual online food handler certificate for a nominal fee that meets many state's requirements. ServSafe takes about an hour to complete and covers five areas: basic food safety; personal hygiene; cross-contamination and allergens; time and temperature; and cleaning and sanitation.

Some considerations to keep in mind when setting up and operating a safe food business in your home kitchen include those below.

- **Wash those hands**

  Hand washing is the first line of defense to prevent the spread of illness-causing bacteria. Wet your hands and rub with soap for at least twenty seconds; sing "Happy Birthday" as a timer and make sure to scrub under your nails where bacteria often dwell. Wash hands before and after handling food, after handling uncooked eggs or after blowing your nose, coughing, sneezing, eating and using the bathroom. When in doubt, wash.

- **Sanitize the prep area**

  Your food preparation area needs to be spotless at all times. Scrub surfaces before and after they come into contact with food, including utensils and cutting boards, using hot, soapy water. Then sanitize. A simple and inexpensive solution of one gallon of water mixed with one tablespoon of bleach will serve as a sanitizing solution to wipe counter surfaces. Place in a well-labeled spray bottle and use on any surfaces that come into contact with food. Let the surfaces air-dry.

  Try some eco-friendly cleaning options and save money and the planet at the same time. Fill a spray bottle with equal parts vinegar and water and use this to clean the top of the stove and appliances. Don't worry about the vinegar smell. It disappears when dry.

- **Separate your cutting boards**
  Use separate cutting boards and plates for produce, meat, poultry, seafood and eggs. Nothing made under cottage food law can contain meat, poultry or seafood, so it's best to keep any of these items you have in your home for personal use sealed and stored separately in the refrigerator.

- **Wash fruits and vegetables thoroughly**
  Run produce under cold water and scrub with a firm produce brush, a food-grade model with sturdy nylon bristles for removing any soil.

Co-author Lisa Kivirist cutting rhubarb stalks to prepare her half pints of Serendipity Rhubarb Shrub for sale at Inn Serendipity. Reaching back to colonial times, shrubs use vinegar and sugar to preserve fruit flavors. JOHN D. IVANKO

- **Keep children out of the kitchen**
  Keep kids out at all times when you cook or bake for the business. Establish firm boundaries in your family between when you are "working" and when things are in "home mode" and the kitchen space goes back to family space. If your children are still young, this may require you to work late at night or early in the morning when they're still sleeping. You could also make arrangements for childcare so you can focus in the kitchen.

- **No pets in the kitchen**
  Check your specific state regulations, as some states do not allow any pets in the home at all if you are operating a cottage food business.

- **Keep insects out**
  Make sure all window and door screens remain in good repair and without any tears to prevent all insects from entering your kitchen workspace.

Lisa Kivirist in the kitchen. JOHN D. IVANKO

- **Make sure your water is safe**
  If using a private well, make sure you annually test your water for coliform bacteria and, possibly, for other chemical contaminants if you live in an area with chemical agriculture.

- **Keep records of each of your product batches**
  Keeping records of your product batches is essential. You can do this by hand in a simple notebook where you record the date, what and how much you made and what ingredients you used. If any issue ever came up regarding your food handling procedures, you will have these logs to reference. We empathize: record-keeping sounds dull and detailed. But records that document the proper procedures you took will show that you employed the highest standards possible should any question arise.

  Most cottage food producers are exempt from the sort of third-party inspections and regulations large food producers must adhere to. However, remember you're still responsible for every last item you make. A written log indicates you take this role seriously.

  Don't agonize, organize. A place for everything and everything in its place makes an efficient and safe kitchen.

11

Make It Legal:

Establish Your Business in 7 Easy Steps

D ON'T LET THE GOVERNMENT, your health department, an insurance agent, a CPA or a family member get in the way of you launching your food business from the kitchen. Avoid letting self-doubt creep in or pangs of fear overwhelm you. You can do it. Thousands of other home cooks have.

We've broken this chapter into seven easy steps to get you going if you live in a state with a cottage food law on the books. While most states have start-up guides for a business, cottage food enterprises can avoid most of the red tape due to your size, lack of employees and limitation on sales.

But to run your business legally — which everyone should do — there are a few federal and state licenses you'll need to get before you sell your first bagel. For a comprehensive list of the regulations, the Small Business Administration (sba.gov) provides an overview with detailed links to state-by-state requirements; go there only if you want to be overwhelmed.

Sure, the national statistic of failed businesses may be nine in ten, but as we pointed out previously, it's practically impossible to fail with a home-based cottage food business since you're starting it in your own kitchen with practically no start-up costs. Your only expenses may be a few licensing fees and the ingredients for the first batch of products you sell. This chapter covers the seven steps necessary to operate, legally, as a business.

Step 1: Do a Local Zoning Check

Just because the state says you can operate a business from your kitchen doesn't mean your county, township or municipality agrees, so check before you go to the next step. Zoning ordinances can be all over the board, vary from one county to the next and sometimes leave a lot of discretionary interpretive control to the administrator in charge. There may be restrictions on everything from the appearance of your home, use of signage or the volume of foot traffic by customers.

Taking Exemptions

Here's the great news. Unless you strike a gold mine with your food product and want to go big, below are some of the many regulatory EXEMPTIONS most cottage food enterprise owners can take, whether or not you're a political libertarian:

- All employee and new hire state regulations. This assumes that you don't hire employees and it's just you in the kitchen, plus your spouse, a family member or kids pitching in from time to time.

- State unemployment insurance, especially in those states that restrict how much the business can gross, and therefore, how much an owner could earn and how often they might be in a position to actually pay themselves a salary.

- State worker's compensation insurance, especially in those states that restrict how much the business can gross.

- USDA's *Food Safety Modernization Act*, because of the products you're allowed to sell under cottage food laws.

- Food and Drug Administration's nutritional labeling, unless you explicitly make a health or nutrition claim or sell wholesale and/or in volumes that exceed their clearly defined exemptions. This exemption includes nutritional analysis and testing. Specifically, per the US FDA:

"One exemption, for low-volume products, applies if the person claiming the exemption employs fewer than an average of 100 full-time equivalent employees and fewer than 100,000 units of that product are sold in the United States in a 12-month period. To qualify for this exemption the person must file a notice annually with FDA.... If a person is not an importer, and has fewer than 10 full-time equivalent employees, that person does not have to file a notice for any food product with annual sales of fewer than 10,000 total units.... If any nutrient content claim (e.g., "sugar free"), health claim, or other nutrition information is provided on the label, or in labeling or advertising, the small business exemption is not applicable for a product."

If in doubt, consult their website (fda.gov).

Some of the above exemptions are based on gross revenues earned, whether you have employees or not, and other variables particular to your state. Be sure to double-check that each of these exemptions applies to your situation

In your conversations or research of the zoning codes in states with more restrictive laws, it's important to convey that you're not starting a huge wholesale enterprise, just a small, direct-to-customer retail operation with a gross sales cap. If the concern is too much traffic at your house, offer to deliver your products to your customers. You may find that you need to bring the zoning administrator up to speed on what a cottage food law even is. If you're in a state that allows wholesale and has no sales cap, just be open with respect to your plans and see what they say.

If you rent an apartment, live in a condo with a condo association or lease a home, you'll also need to read the fine print in your lease or agreement and see if there's anything explicitly preventing you from running a business out of your kitchen or your rented home. The same holds true if you happen to live in a planned residential neighborhood or complex; check with the homeowners' association before you proceed.

In each scenario above, based on your research and to cover your bases, make sure you write down the specifics of any conversations that give you the green light, including the name of the person you talked with, when and exactly what was said. Try to get as much as you can in writing, since you can call upon this information later should an issue arise. E-mail works great for documentation if you choose to use this method of correspondence.

Step 2: Get Licensed by Your State's Department of Agriculture

Contact the governmental office that deals with the cottage food law for your state, usually the department of agriculture, though the regulations vary a lot from state to state. Your state's health department is not the administrative or regulatory body that licenses and enforces cottage food law; they handle restaurants, catering operations and other facilities where food is "prepared" and "served." For a quick and updated reference, see our book's website for the latest state-by-state cottage food developments and contact information.

In most cases, you'll need to file for a "cottage food license," occasionally called a "home food processor" license. A nominal fee may be charged in some cases. Some states will require an on-site inspection of your kitchen facilities while others call for some form of food-handling training. As covered previously, ServSafe Certification is one such online or classroom-based nationally accredited program set up by the National Restaurant Association; it's often used by the restaurant industry to make sure their employees understand basic food safety practices for preparing and serving food.

Step 3: Set Up Your Business and Structure it Wisely

By now, you have a name for your business, plus another fictional name (i.e., doing business as or DBA), both covered in Chapter 4. Next is setting up your business. There are several ways to do so, addressed in more detail in our *ECOpreneuring* book. You'll need to evaluate your own situation, your tolerance for risk and your business to determine which works best for you.

While cottage food entrepreneurs sell non-hazardous foods, there is a possibility that something might not be just right with your product, no fault of your own. Maybe one of your ingredients was mislabeled; perhaps a sliver of a nutshell found its way into the bag of walnuts you used for your granola. It happens. If a customer breaks a tooth or chokes on this shell, you could be held liable for damages. By operating as a corporation or LLC, you may be shielded from possible issues on a personal level.

Depending on your comfort level, you may be best off leaving the details and specifics of setting up your business to a certified public accountant (CPA) or a business attorney. While all business structures require governmental record-keeping and forms to be filed, corporations and limited liability companies (LLCs) involve additional legal and accounting requirements. That said, many cottage food operators we've interviewed have found the process straightforward enough that they did it themselves.

Below are several common business structures, broken down by the most recognized reason for choosing one over another: personal liability protection. This is a shield that prevents anyone with a court judgment or financial claims against the business to touch anything other than the assets of the corporation or LLC. In other words, certain business structures protect the personal assets of the officers, stockholders and employees of the business, reducing the risk that your house, personal property or bank accounts could be seized as a part of a court settlement.

No Personal Liability Protection
Sole Proprietorship

By far the most common, easiest and least costly business structure is a self-employed sole owner or sole proprietorship. Income from the business is reported as a part of the owner's personal income using the IRS Schedule C or Schedule C-EZ; you may be subject to self-employment taxes of 15.3 percent. You are responsible for the liabilities and debts of the business. If your business is sued, everything you own could be threatened by the lawsuit.

General Partnership

If you go into business with a sibling or other family member, you would do so as a partnership instead of as a sole proprietor. When there are two or more individuals who are owners of a for-profit business, typically operating under a written partnership agreement, the business is a general partnership. All partners are responsible for the liabilities and debts of the business. Income is reported on the IRS Schedule K-1 and may be subject to 15.3 percent self-employment tax. The partnership must file an annual return, Form 1065, with the federal government and possibly a state return.

Distinct Legal Entity Offering Personal Liability Protection to Shareholders
S Corporation, or Sub-chapter S Corporation

Essentially a tax accounting classification, an S corporation is a common stock-issuing legal entity, income

Officers, Shareholders and Taking Stock

Unlike a sole proprietorship, a corporation or LLC is a distinct legal entity, with a corporate formality that separates the owners of the company, the shareholders and its advisory body, the board of directors and its officers (president, secretary, treasurer) and managerial body, the chief executive officer (CEO) and the chief financial officer.

By law, a corporation must maintain a registered office and agent within the state where it is formed to respond to legal and official matters. If your corporation is in the same state as your residence, you can be your own resident agent. A one-person or family corporation must still follow the formality of corporate procedures related to decision-making and meetings. Document the "meeting" with corporate minutes, even if that means you write down your decisions if you're the only board member as well as the CEO, president, secretary and treasurer in a one-person-owned corporation.

Ownership of the company is signified by receipt of stock certificates reflecting financial, property or service contributions to the business; shares can be voting or non-voting, common or preferred; the latter acts similarly to a bond in terms of its value. Shareholders taking stock usually have voting rights, financial distributions rights to dividends if declared by the board of directors and proportionate rights to assets should the corporation be dissolved.

from which is taxed only once when it passes through to the employees or shareholders of the corporation on their personal income tax return. Like C corporations, discussed next, S corporations must file articles of incorporation, hold director and shareholder meetings, file an annual corporation tax return, keep corporate minutes and vote on corporate decisions. Most S corporations can use the more straightforward cash method of accounting whereby income is taxed when received and expenses are deductible when paid. Unlike C corporations, S corporations are limited in the number of shareholders they can have.

Limited Liability Company

The limited liability company (LLC) is a separate legal entity established by filing articles of LLC formulation or similar documents in the state where it is formed. The number of LLC members, various classes of stock and tax accounting selection determine a diversity of avenues to properly meet tax liabilities, whether the LLC is treated as a partnership or a C or S corporation.

C Corporation

The most expensive and complex of business structures, the C corporation is a legal entity set up within a given state and owned by shareholders of its issued stock. It's unlikely, due to the scale of your operation, that you'd form a C corporation — unless, of course, you strike it rich and turn your products into a full-blown big-time business, a possibility we cover in the Scaling Up section of this book.

The corporation, not the shareholders or directors, is responsible for the debt and liabilities of the

Affordable Legal Documents

Some states have very straightforward forms that must be completed to set up small businesses as a corporation or LLC. Others, less so. Below are a couple of low-cost options to consider if you want to structure your business as either. Of course, if you tend to be risk adverse and have the funds, you may feel most comfortable hiring an attorney licensed in your state who specializes in small business legal issues.

- **Nolo Press**
  nolo.com
  One of the Internet's leading websites offering free and easy-to-understand legal information and various do-it-yourself products.

- **LegalZoom**
  legalzoom.com
  For as little as $99, plus state fees, this online company can help you set up your enterprise as a LLC or subchapter S corporation in most states. It could be a source for other legal documents, too.

C corporation. C corporations must file articles of incorporation, hold director and shareholder meetings, file an annual corporation tax return, keep corporate minutes and vote on corporate decisions. Income from C corporations, after expenses have been deducted, is taxed both at the corporate level and at the individual level, on wages and dividends paid to shareholders.

Regardless of the structure of your business, you will need to file some form of annual state and federal tax returns, using either the FEIN for your business or your social security number if you're a sole proprietor.

Step 4: Secure a State Business License

The state in which you live wants to know if someone is operating a business there. For those of you who are merely diversifying your already established business by selling products through the cottage food law, you should have already completed this step.

For everyone else, you'll need to contact your state's department of revenue (or equivalent) to complete a simple application and pay a fee for the privilege of being in business for yourself. If your business is incorporated, a LLC, a partnership or a sole proprietorship operated under a fictitious or trade name (i.e, DBA, doing business as), there is a specific fee for your business license. If you operate as a sole proprietorship under your own name, you may not need to get a license. Verify what your state requires of you.

Step 5: Get a State Sales Tax Permit

Now that you're selling something to the public, your state's department of revenue may require your business to collect sales tax on certain "value-added" products, like pickles or wedding cakes. To do so, you'll need to get a sales tax permit and understand the state and, possibly, county and city taxes associated with every one of those

Federal Employer Identification Number (FEIN)

If you end up setting up a corporation, LLC or business partnership or find yourself hiring employees, you'll need to get a federal employer identification number (FEIN) from the US Internal Revenue Service. You can apply for this number through the IRS on the Internet (irs.gov) or by filing the IRS form SS-4. The FEIN is sometimes referred to as an EIN, Employer Tax ID or a tax identification number or TIN; they're the same thing.

12-ounce packages of granola or gift tins of stollen that you sell at the Christkindlmarkt in December.

Heads up. In the government's move to make everything electronic (except voting), many states are requiring Internet-based access and payment for related filings and fees. If you have little computer know-how, you may need to see if your local library can help you with this process.

Step 6: Get a Local Business License (If Needed)

On the local or municipal level, some cities or counties may require you to have a business license or tax certificate before you can operate. A call to your city or county's clerk's office will lay this one to rest.

Step 7: Manage Risk with Insurance

Living is risky business. Cars slide off the road after hitting a patch of ice, products stop working and bones break. When you go into business selling a food product, you're accepting an additional amount of risk. You could be held liable for someone getting sick from eating your product, perhaps at no fault of your own. Today's headlines are filled with outbreaks of E. coli-tainted vegetables and salmonella-laced peanut butter, largely a result of an increasingly industrialized food system. Major product recalls are about as regular as oil changes on your car.

Generally speaking, the cottage food industry is the antithesis of our industrial food system. It's likely that you're the only person preparing the entire order of marmalade or macaroons. You personally select each and every ingredient, knead and mince as needed, then bake, simmer or hot bath. You're the one packing your product. Delivering it, too. Most of what you sell may travel less than twenty miles.

What we find in our supposedly "safe" supermarket travels thousands of miles, can be highly processed and is filled with artificial ingredients and preservatives thanks to the magic of modern chemistry. But the ingredients listed on your package can be pronounced; they're real, minimally processed and made locally.

If you scale up and sell wholesale to regional grocery stores or a national specialty food chain, it's different, covered in greater detail in the Scaling Up section. You may even be required to have a "recall" plan in place for your product. Plus, once your product is out of your hands, you don't have control over how the distributor or retailer handles it, spawning the growth of "tamper-proof" packaging.

What if your product gets left in a distribution truck that breaks down in the desert for two days? What if a retailer decides to display your preserves in direct sunlight in a south-facing front window? Of course, you would want to avoid such extreme heat or sunlight conditions on your products. But what if? That's what insurance is for: covering you for accidents, the unknown or situations beyond your control.

Regardless of your approach to your ingredients, products, customers and scale of operations, there's always a possibility something may not go exactly as planned. In response to our litigious society, insurance has become a necessary part of both living and doing business.

What you need to evaluate is your appetite for risk and the insurance requirements related to what you want to do with your business. You should start by checking if you are already covered in some way, either through your existing homeowner's insurance or in how you structure your business (covered in Step 3 of this chapter). To manage risk, consider combining insurance with other strategies. Of course, your "non-hazardous" products themselves are another way you reduce your risk exposure.

If you're already in business, then you're probably already covered at some level for food or personal liability issues. In most cases, it's nothing more than checking with your insurance company.

For example, for our small B&B (and cottage food enterprise), we have the business specifically listed on our homeowner's insurance policy as a rider; the annual premium is less than $100 and provides $300,000 of personal liability coverage. Our business is viewed as "incidental to the home" by our insurer, Cincinnati Insurance Company. Additionally, we have a $1 million umbrella insurance policy that covers anything we do on our property and in our car, above and beyond the $300,000 coverage. Everything changes should we decide at some point to prepare food products in a rented commercial kitchen; at that point, we'd need to purchase a commercial business liability policy that may run, at minimum, over $500 per year.

If you're just hanging out your shingle, you'll need to explore with an insurance company what level and type of coverage might be needed for you to feel comfortable and sleep well at night. The annual premium for

"Starting a cottage food operation has huge legal ramifications, and cottage food laws accidentally make people think they are shielded from rules and regulations. I have concerns about whether cottage foods actually increase potential liability and about the insure-ability of the operations. I've heard of folks getting dropped by insurance companies or trouble finding an affordable quote. This has to do with insurance agents not fully understanding what these laws entail and the small scale that we're talking about. Many are going without insurance at all. The state laws authorize you to sell certain foods but do not cover nor exempt you from liability issues."

— RACHEL ARMSTRONG, AN ATTORNEY AND EXECUTIVE DIRECTOR OF FARM COMMONS (FARMCOMMONS.ORG), PROVIDING LEGAL EDUCATION FOR THE SUSTAINABLE AGRICULTURE COMMUNITY. CHECK OUT THE FARM COMMONS WEBSITE FOR VARIOUS FREE WEBINARS AND RESOURCES THAT DIAL DEEPER INTO LEGAL ISSUES RELATED TO VALUE-ADDED PRODUCTS.

your business and product liability coverage will depend on the level of coverage, sales venue, gross sales volume and, of course, your products themselves. In many cases, a commercial insurance policy will be required not for your state, but for the venues where you sell your products. Many sales venues require a "certificate of insurance" for an amount ranging from $300,000 to $1 million; this certificate, generated by your agent based on your policy, explicitly refers to the venue by name.

In response to the growing number of businesses and sole proprietorships in the food industry, Utah-based Veracity Insurance Solutions offers a Food Liability Insurance Program (fliprogram.com) with an annual premium that starts at less than $300. At this rate, the company offers a general liability policy limited to $2 million.

As discussed previously, structuring your business from the start as a corporation or LLC offers a liability benefit but comes at a cost and with more complicated paperwork. Maintaining adequate insurance coverage would add to your protection.

The challenge remains finding a balance between the joy and financial benefits of operating a food-based enterprise and managing some of the risks associated with doing so. In the end, it's your decision. But keep in mind that, in nearly all cases, cottage food laws by their very definition apply to non-hazardous food products. Enough said.

12

Day-to-Day Financial Management

W**ITHOUT BEING TOO CUMBERSOME,** boring or filled with pages of numbers, this chapter covers the day-to-day financial aspects of your enterprise. As a CFO, your success is practically guaranteed. You just need to load up the minivan with your cookies, keep track of your sales and smile on the way to the bank at the end of the day to deposit your profits. But as a CFO, you also need to be a chief financial officer for your enterprise, and that means keeping track of the finances.

To be legitimately in business, you need to make at least some profit at least three of the last five years, according to the IRS. As we'll cover next, business revenue minus expenses equals profit. For most cottage food enterprises, it's rarely a matter of if they'll be profitable. Rather, by how much?

Day-to-Day Financial Management

Even if you think you hate numbers or dread balancing your checkbook, you can keep track of your revenues (sales) and any expenses related to your operation as a business. It's just a matter of coming up with an easy process that works for you.

Again: business revenue minus expenses equals profit. It's this profit that the IRS must see on either your personal tax return or that of your LLC or corporation during three of the last five years for your enterprise to be considered a for-profit business and not a hobby. According to the IRS, someone operating a hobby cannot deduct any expenses.

Going right to the source, on the IRS website:

> *an activity qualifies as a business if it is carried on with the reasonable expectation of earning a profit.... The IRS presumes that an activity is carried on for profit if it makes a profit during at least three of the last five tax years, including the current year.*

So you don't need to make a profit every year. The business loss that results in a year where expenses exceed revenues can be claimed on your personal tax return and may end up reducing your income tax liability if you have other sources of income, say from your full-time job, interest income from savings accounts or dividend income from stocks. For more clarification on this, consult with a CPA or other tax professional.

We'll leave the discussion of non-profit organizations for our *ECO-preneuring* book, since technically, you could set up your business as a non-profit with your proceeds benefiting the organization's mission and goals.

Making and Taking Money

Revenue is the money earned by your business, also called gross sales or income. Before your first sale is made, you'll need to open a business checking account, separate from your personal checking account. Co-mingling

How the Patriot Act Changed How We Bank

When the *PATRIOT ACT* passed after the tragedy of 9/11, it transformed how banking is done in the US, in part to intercept and obstruct terrorism. Now more than ever, your banking business is government business.

As a result, to open a checking account for your business, you'll need the following if your business is a corporation or LLC:

- a copy of the articles of incorporation for your business;
- Federal Employer Identification Number (FEIN) or Tax Identification Number (TIN);
- the minutes from a board meeting that explicitly states the representatives of the business who are authorized to access the bank account;

- a resolution that states who is authorized on the account (a blank form to be completed, usually provided by the bank).

If your business is a sole proprietorship or partnership, you'll likely need the following:

- Social Security number (SSN);
- some form of statement or note, perhaps generated on your company letterhead, that explicitly states the person or persons associated with the business who are authorized to access the bank account;
- a resolution that states who is authorized on the account (a blank form to be completed, usually provided by the bank).

The above requirements may vary slightly from bank to bank, so check with your local bank.

business and personal money is the easiest way to lose track of what you're earning and draw the unnecessary and unwanted attention and scrutiny of the IRS.

When you sell a jar of pickles, just deposit the proceeds from that sale into your business account and you're good to go. When you have an expense, pay for it with a check from this account, creating a nice paper trail for the IRS to follow. If your business warrants it, consider taking out a business credit card for purchases made for your enterprise; this allows you to track and account for your business expenses and avoids having to use your personal credit card for business purchases. The more transparent you can make it for the IRS, the better.

Before your first sale, figure out how to receive payment. Cash works great; it won't bounce and it's simple to deposit. Depending on your community, personal checks can add additional flexibility, since some people may not walk around with wads of cash. For those CFOs selling to corporate accounts or special events like weddings, not only will checks be the only way to go, you'll likely need to crunch a simple invoice for payment. Be prepared to generate a receipt as well.

These days, some of the customers eager to buy your products may not use either cash or checks much. It's a decision you'll likely face: a customer who wants your products but can only buy them on credit. Credit and debit cards, thanks to their convenience and widespread use, have become the de facto way people pay for things. The question then becomes, are the additional sales made possible by accepting credit cards worth the fees you'll be charged for each transaction? Of course, these fees are legitimate business expenses, covered later in this chapter.

You don't need a full-blown merchant account with cumbersome contracts and expensive scanning machines to accept a credit card payment for a dozen donuts; these expensive, complicated and ever-changing systems may be best left for larger companies with sales volume to support it.

Following are some of the many credit card-processing options where you only pay a nominal fee based on a percentage of the charge. Thanks to the proliferation of mobile devices, smartphones and computers, plus Internet or cellular connections, processing credit cards has become easier and more widespread. Most companies offering "card readers," small devices that can read a swiped credit card, also provide an option to manually key in the credit card number, but charge a higher percentage fee and fixed transaction cost for this feature.

- **PayPal: paypal.com**
  Among the most widely used, secure and safe ways to receive payment via credit cards or through someone's PayPal account via the computer, tablet or smartphone. No contracts or monthly service fees; just a percentage fee and a charge deducted for each transaction completed. PayPal offers a mobile app and card reader for payments on the go.

- **Square: squareup.com**
  Using a free Square device that plugs into the phone jack on your smartphone, tablet or computer, you can swipe the card and complete your checkout from just about anywhere.

- **Spark Pay: sparkpay.com**
  The free card reader from Capital One Bank can process credit cards on a smartphone, tablet or computer using wireless and mobile devices.

Money Belt or Drawer

You'll discover few people can pay with the exact change. Depending on the sales venue, customers may arrive fresh from a cash station with twenties or fifties in their wallets or purses.

To cover your cash sales, you'll need to have a system for making change. A money belt or cash drawer, besides being convenient, helps avoid bills and change being placed in your pockets or coat jackets in the flurry of business transactions. A shoebox can be used in a pinch, but think about the mess of money that piles up in a shoebox and the message it conveys to customers about your level of professionalism.

For small-time operators, getting a system to manage your money when you're doing events helps keep you organized. If you're the type of person who needs to know exactly how many muffins and what flavors sold, keep a tally sheet at your booth and track each sale. For a less detailed summary, you can just add up what you didn't sell and subtract it from what you made to arrive at your sales total, then subtract the variable costs that went into your order to get your profit for the event. You'll miss some details about your volume discount doing it this way, but your profit at the end of the day will be the same.

Income Statement and Balance Sheet

Eventually, the financial activities of your business are organized into an income statement, also called a profit and loss statement (P&L), with revenues at the top and expenses at the bottom. Your business can also be summarized by a balance sheet reflecting the assets and liabilities (and equity) of the business. Come tax time, your CPA or tax preparation professional will help you sort out your balance sheet, with the difference between assets and liabilities being the net worth of your business. Most small businesses are set up to have a calendar year rather than a fiscal year, that is, a period of twelve months starting at some date during the calendar year.

Chances are, due to your small scale, that you'll only need to tabulate these records once, at the end of your calendar year, when you prepare your state and federal tax returns. If you have to pay sales taxes, you may even be able to file these on an annual basis instead of quarterly, monthly or weekly. When in doubt, request to be exempted or allowed to file on an annual basis by your state regulatory agency, to cut down on your (and their) paperwork.

Expenses Defined

There are many financial benefits of becoming a business, depending on how you structure it. Not only are businesses taxed after their expenses have been deducted, but many legitimate deductions are available to small business that reduce its reported earnings. The IRS tax code specifies the following related to business expenses:

> *IRS Code Section 162(a), Trade or business expenses:*
> *"There shall be allowed as a deduction all the ordinary and necessary expenses paid or incurred during the taxable year in carrying on any trade or business."*
> *IRS Code Section 212, Expenses for production of income:*
> *"In the case of an individual, there shall be allowed as a deduction all the ordinary and necessary expenses paid or incurred during the taxable year."*

"The [cottage food] law allows entrepreneurs to start a business without going into great debt. It allowed them to try their hand, so to speak — and then if their business did well, they could know they had an idea that could be successful, and some profits to start their own company."

— Jeannie Nichols, Michigan State University Extension

Be "fair and reasonable" in your business expenses. You can't deduct a family trip to Hawaii. However, deducting a trip and related expenses to attend the Summer Fancy Food Show in New York City seems fair and reasonable, so long as your trip involves researching products, developing your marketing plan, reaching out to potential wholesalers and so forth; document who you meet and what you accomplish.

Some of the more common deductible business expenses include the following:

Supplies and Ingredients

From canning jars to product ingredients, any expenses associated with your product, its production, labeling and packaging can be deducted.

Government Licenses and Fees

Any fees associated with compliance with governmental regulations and licenses are deductible.

Credit Card Processing Fees

Starting at around 2.7% per transaction, if you accept credit cards or other forms of payment beyond cash and checks, these fees can be deducted.

Advertising

From printing costs for flyers or a banner to website hosting plans, if you spend money on advertising to make money, it's deductible.

Use of Your Personal Vehicle for the Business

Owners of vehicles who use these for business purposes can deduct those miles associated with business use and be reimbursed for mileage by the business. For example, when you drive to sell your products at a booth at a local event, you can reimburse yourself at the IRS-specified rate; if it's a 30-mile round trip, your business would reimburse you, as the owner of the car used for business purposes, 30 miles times the IRS mileage rate established for that year. Pay yourself by business check to create a paper trail for the IRS. Make sure to maintain a vehicle travel mileage log for each vehicle used for business purposes; in this log you simply record the date, purpose of the business trip and the starting and ending odometer reading. Note that when you take those business miles as a deduction, you cannot also deduct actual gas or diesel fuel purchases, or any car repairs or maintenance.

Employee Training

Direct expenses related to culinary training, educational programs or workshops or other ways you might endeavor to improve your skills and receive technical information on managing your business are deductible. Be sure to document these class, workshop or course expenses with a receipt for payment; file those class notes as backup, should the IRS want to know what you learned. A ServSafe "safe food handling" course would fall under this expense category.

Use of Premise for Business Purposes Only

Here's the bad news: paying yourself rent for the use of your kitchen for business purposes is NOT acceptable because you also use this space for personal use. However, if you decide to use a home office exclusively for business, perhaps to fulfill orders, print out flyers or conduct other aspects of your business, you can deduct the corresponding portion of the square footage of the property as a business rental expense, plus the corresponding portion of utilities, insurance, repairs and taxes.

Based on the fair market value of a local rental property for office space, you can establish the rental rate for the use of your personal property (i.e., a room in your home for a home office) and pay yourself rent for such use by the business. Of course, you need to set up a simple rental agreement between yourself, as the homeowner or property owner, and the business to have on file as documentation for the IRS. Just for kicks, it wouldn't hurt to take a nice clear picture of your home office, too.

Equipment and Capital Expenses

Some investments, like a brand-new mixer for your bakery business, are considered capital expenses and reflected as assets on your balance sheet. Rather than deducting them, you must capitalize them as long-term investments. These assets, however, can be depreciated, reducing reported earnings.

Depreciation

Business assets wear out, break down and become obsolete, especially with the rapid advancements in technology. The IRS allows a non-cash deductible business expense of depreciation to account for the loss of value over time for assets owned by the business. Depreciation reduces the reported

earnings of the business. The amount of depreciation and its duration varies by the type of asset.

For more details on deductions, review some of the Nolo Press books and their website (nolo.org). For an overwhelming headache, visit the IRS website (irs.gov) for the latest updates and changes to the tax code, then consider contracting the services of a certified public accountant who specializes in small business returns. As a bonus, the CPA fee is a tax-deductible business expense; however, making an error on your tax return and penalties for doing so are not.

Bookkeeping Basics

We know you want to be in the kitchen, decorating cakes or simmering your pizza sauce — not adding up numbers or itemizing receipts. Since you're in business, however, you'll need to keep track of the money coming in and going out of the business. It's called bookkeeping, for short.

As a CFO, you can keep track of sales and expenses with a ledger, either electronically with a computer or tablet or the old-fashioned way by writing them down by hand. You can also use your ledger to record transactions related to assets, liabilities and owners' equity. There are numerous tablet-based bookkeeping apps. For the more computer-savvy crowd, Intuit's popular Quickbooks (quickbooks.com) may suffice, but you may find these too detailed and expensive for your needs, at least when you're just starting out.

To keep records for your business, you can put your sales receipts in one folder, box or cabinet drawer, by month, quarter or year, depending on the scale of your operations. If you don't have a receipt system, just create a simple receipt on paper with the date, customer/event and total sales. For expenses, hang onto every receipt, from your start-up costs to ingredient purchases, again, organized by month, quarter or year. These receipts are proof that you're in business. You don't have to make it any harder than this.

Two methods can be used for accounting, the process by which financial information is recorded, summarized and interpreted. The more commonly used and straightforward "cash basis" of accounting establishes that income is taxable when received and expenses are deductible when paid. The more complex "accrual basis" method records payments or expenses when they're agreed upon, which may take place at some future date; cash may not have been received or spent by the business. Most CFOs opt for cash basis accounting due to its simplicity.

There's no cooking the books for CFOs, though. Keep everything on the up and up. Go out of your way to deposit every last cent of revenue you earn and document your fair and reasonable business expenses.

Cash Flow Is King

Cash flow is simply the cash received and spent by your business over a specific period of time, usually a year. Some cash is essential to getting your

Cash flow Projections for Inn Serendipity FRESH BAKED

Inn Serendipity® FRESH BAKED

Item	Jan	Feb	Mar	Apr	May	Jun	Jul	Aug	Sep	Oct	Nov	Dec	TOTALS
Sales (forecasted)													
- Special Orders			35	45	190	250	220	300	225	90	45	15	1,415
- Events				325						580		150	1,055
TOTAL SALES	0	0	35	370	190	250	220	300	225	670	45	165	2,470
Expenses													
- License Fees	10	25											35
- Ingredients		35	20	55	34	35	40	25	20	95	10	20	389
- Flyers Printing		20											20
- Booth Fees				25						200		35	260
- Business Miles	40	45	30	40	25	35	35	25	25	45	20	45	410
- Credit Card Fees				12		10		3		34	2	13	74
TOTAL EXPENSES	50	125	50	132	59	80	75	53	45	374	32	113	1,188
Starting Cash	300	250	125	110	348	479	649	794	1,041	1,221	1,517	1,530	
Ending Cash Balance	250	125	110	348	479	649	794	1,041	1,221	1,517	1,530	1,582	

As we wait for Wisconsin legislators to turn our Cookie Bill into a law so we can sell our home-baked goods to the public and expand our operations, we wanted to forecast what our cash flow might be when we start our business. The following serves as an example by month, starting with a $300 cash balance. Sales revenue minus expenses results in a net gain or loss in cash in any given month. By the end of the year, based on the sales projections and expense estimates, our cash balance would increase to $1,582.

business up and going, though with cottage food enterprises, you don't need much.

It's essential that you don't run out of money while customers are still discovering your great-tasting products. It's possible that there's a seasonality to your sales, meaning you may be rolling in the bucks around the holidays but light for several months in the summer. Account for seasonality and allow some time to get your business established. It may take longer than you imagine for customers to discover your products.

A cash flow projection includes both anticipated cash receipts from sales on a monthly or quarterly basis and cash disbursements for expenses, including cost of goods sold (direct costs related to your products), marketing, license fees, delivery costs and equipment. The goal is to avoid or minimize any periods where you have a net negative cash balance.

No Cakewalk

Starting and operating your own business, even a small one, takes time, energy, perseverance, hard work and a little money. As in life, your business may have ups and downs, recipe flops and customers who may be challenging to work with or bounce a check. However, if you follow the advice and guidance offered throughout this book, you'll hopefully sidestep most of the trapdoors and find enough of the secret passageways to make your way along on your journey so that it's fun, satisfying, meaningful and financially rewarding.

Once you get going, you may find that some aspects of operating the business are less enjoyable. Making sales calls to solicit possible corporate events, invoicing a company for a delivery of cookies, preparing and signing a contract for an expensive decorated wedding cake, posting updates on Facebook or following up an e-mail campaign with potential customers may diminish some of the enjoyment of operating your food enterprise. Don't let it.

To cope, stick to your strengths. Focus on what you love about your business and explore ways to operate it that are true to your priorities and values. Just because "everyone" is on Facebook doesn't mean you have to be. Find what works for you. If you're fortunate to find people eager to help you with your enterprise, go with your instincts and invite them to help out; just be mindful of the legal requirements if you decide to take on bona fide employees.

One thing is for sure: expect the unexpected. Don't be shocked the day before your first big order that your reliable car suddenly has a flat tire — or your oven goes on the blink after an early morning thunderstorm. Even if disruptive events never happen, having a plan in place and anticipating setbacks or issues, like power outages, will allow you to weather most storms that come your way.

Consider having some contingency plans, like a backup option for a car — or a taxi number on file. While an extended service contract for a home oven may seem excessive, if you're a slightly risk-adverse home bakery owner, take one out for this heavily used appliance anyway. You may live to regret it if you don't.

In the end, you define the success of your business. No one else does. And don't lose sight of why you became a cottage food entrepreneur in the first place.

Co-author Lisa Kivirist and her son Liam at a farmers' market. John D. Ivanko

Scaling Up

SECTION 4

13

Scaling Up

PERHAPS YOU'RE HITTING YOUR STATE'S COTTAGE FOOD SALES CAP. Or discovered that your product is not just great, it's awesome. Maybe you're getting hounded by specialty food stores that can't wait to stock your mandel bread, as soon as you can sell wholesale. On a personal level, perhaps you want to scale up your operations because you're having so much fun and like the thrill and excitement of running your own enterprise. Maybe you increasingly find making scones more enjoyable than your current job that confines you to a cubicle; you desire a full-time food venture based in a kitchen. Then this chapter is for you.

Part of the attraction to and purpose of cottage food laws is to give entrepreneurs a chance to test the market before sinking thousands, or hundreds of thousands, of dollars into an idea. It reduces the risk and jump-starts innovation and small business. As we write in *ECOpreneuring* and throughout the pages of this book, we believe anyone can be a small business owner and make a living for themselves by following their passions and dreams rather than earning a living clocking in at a job. Life's too short not to do what you love and create a life worth living.

Whether you want to take it to the next level to see if you can hit the jackpot, or at least earn a full-time livelihood with your passion and talent for cooking, we'll begin this section of the book by pressing a pause button to encourage some contemplation. Then we'll summarize the next steps if you decide to scale up your enterprise and point you in the direction of books, websites and other resources that might help.

In most cases, scaling up takes place along a continuum, from the cottage food entry level with its various limitations all the way up to a multi-million-dollar company that could even, one day, be gobbled up by a multinational food conglomerate like Unilever.

First, a Reality Check

Scaling up your operations can be as fulfilling as running your small cottage food enterprise, except the potential payout and profits could be much higher. With this financial freedom, however, comes the regulatory super storm, depending on where you rest on the continuum of expansion. Operating under a $10,000 sales cap is considerably different from wholesaling to a regional Whole Foods Market.

The challenges of expansion are hardly insurmountable — there are thousands of food businesses out there thriving, after all. You just need to be aware that much of what we have covered so far in this book about regulations, licenses, UPC codes and nutritional labeling for food products may be out the door, depending on how much you're scaling up.

Before jumping in with both feet, revisit your goals, objectives and aspirations for your business — and your life. How much time do you want to spend cooking, cleaning, canning or delivering product? How do you feel about hiring the employees you'll probably need to expand the business? Or will you subcontract some aspects of the business that you either find yourself avoiding or feel need more attention, like bookkeeping, website development, social media or sales?

Many hired hands make light work for your stepped-up production. Now that you've moved beyond a cottage food enterprise, perhaps finding the need to make hundreds of loaves of your Honey Hearth Bread for a regional grocery store, you're going to need some help. Instead of kneading the bread yourself, you'll now be managing other bakers and trying to make sure they do it as well as you do. Ditto for your new sales force and delivery person. You're an owner-manager now, no longer the cook in the kitchen.

This distinction between "bread baker" and "bread baking manager" is a big and important one to consider. Did you get into doing this because you love having your hands in the dough? Do you get a real kick out of talking to your loyal customers every week at the farmers' market? If so, think carefully about the expansion and its potential to separate you from the very process of baking or canning, or other aspect of the business that you enjoy. Instead of keeping an eye on the oven, you may find your face in front of the computer screen managing orders, inventory and payroll.

Outside of business considerations, what does your family think? To take it the next level, are you giving your notice at the company you've worked at for the last decade and if so, do you have a plan for healthcare or retirement? Do you have enough "emergency funds" to cover the mortgage or car payments while you're expanding?

These can, and should, be heady questions, requiring some soul-searching. As you grow your enterprise, risk, failure, liability issues, employer responsibility and complexity grow with it. You may find, too, that the expectations of your customers also change, becoming more demanding, requiring a higher level of service, even more exacting consistency. Depending on how much you expand, chances are you'll no longer be on a first-name basis with them either.

If you've never worked in the kitchen of a restaurant or catering company, you may find yourself staring at commercial equipment you have no idea how to operate. And your recipes, how do you prepare them in a 20-quart mixer, so big it sits on the floor and resembles an inverted R2D2?

Before proceeding, it's time to yank out that back-of-a-napkin business plan, punch a pot of coffee and put onto paper a polished, fifty-page-plus business plan with sales projections, a more detailed marketing plan and so forth. Now that you're investing some serious cash, time and energy, it's time to make sure that you're pulling a salary (the government requires it!) and have some profits left over at the end of the day.

Casting Off the Shackles of the Cottage Food Law

In a commercial kitchen, there's nothing you can't make. How about cakes with cream cheese frosting? Yep! Blueberry sour cream pies? Ditto. Both will require refrigeration and a host of other factors when you sell them to the public, but the point is, you can. You can even make chicken pot pies for the frozen counter or fresh-daily Tex-Mex burrito wraps for resale at the local convenience store.

You can make anything you want in that commercial kitchen, depending on the classification of your permit and what that kitchen facility is authorized to make. And with the license comes the litany of regulations and product safety precautions you must make before anyone even gets to take one bite.

Wholesale Expansion

So, the time has arrived to scale up. To be clear, your business is going to get more complicated and costly and demand a level of commitment far beyond what you put into your small cottage food enterprise.

While you may continue to sell directly to the public, the rules change at this stage for the various other sales venues open to you, including wholesale and mail order. As mentioned earlier, your production must take place in a licensed commercial kitchen appropriate for the type of product you sell.

State Prerequisites for Wholesale and Mail Order

Most states have two prerequisites for producing your food product for wholesale and/or mail order:

(a) Food Processor Permit or License

A food processor permit is the state-approved documentation and training that proves and legitimizes that you can safely produce a specified item with

So, You Want to Grow Big

Many aspects and options related to scaling up your enterprise are summarized briefly in this chapter and the next, provided as a tool for you to consider as you contemplate your next phase.

Homemade for Sale was explicitly written for the small-scale, home kitchen-based food entrepreneur. While much of the marketing and business management chapters are as applicable to small operations as they are to large ones, the following books and other resources will serve as a guide beyond the basics covered in the final two chapters.

• *From Kitchen to Market: Selling Your Gourmet Food Specialty* by Stephen F. Hall
The authoritative book on getting a specialty food product to as wide a market as possible is paired with a dynamic website (specialty-foodresource.com) that picks up where Hall's book leaves off.

• *How to Start a Home-based Bakery Business* by Detra Denay Davis
Focusing exclusively on a bakery business, Davis' book covers, in a little more detail, issues related to scaling up your operations.

• *Starting a Part-time Food Business: Everything You Need to Know to Turn Your Love of Food into a Successful Business Without Necessarily Quitting Your Day Job* by Jennifer Lewis.
A straightforward look at what you may need to do to take your business up another notch.

• *The Soup to Nuts Small Business Tradeshow Guide: What Every Artisan, Craftsman, and Handmade Entrepreneur Needs to Know About Growing Their Wholesale Business Through Tradeshows* by Jennifer Lewis. Take the mystery out of exhibiting at a food-focused trade show. If you're going big, you're going to need some bucks to connect with retailers who are looking for products that will sell on their shelves.

the intent to sell to the public. In other words, it's the necessary process to prove to your state that you can legally and safely produce your product.

Generally speaking, the more foods are processed, the more tightly they're regulated. The more steps involved in making your item and the longer the list of ingredients, the more complicated the regulations are. Note the exact title of such a license varies by state; it may be called a "retail food license," a "food processor permit," "processed food business license" or something similar, meaning basically the same thing.

Additionally, there may be different layers of licenses depending on exactly what you are producing and to whom you are selling. States often distinguish wholesale in a separate licensing category with specific requirements and procedures. For example, in Wisconsin, you would need a "retail food establishment license" to sell direct to consumers (including Internet sales) and a "food processing plant license" to sell wholesale.

There may also be federal requirements and additional labeling requirements, depending on what you are producing. But once you receive your wholesale license, the doors of opportunity open wide. You can sell your products anywhere in the United States and to anyone, including larger retail outlets and via mail order across state lines.

(b) Licensed Food Production Facility

The type of food processor permit you receive will determine the type of commercial facility in which you must process your product. Commercial kitchens are not all treated the same by state regulators. What you're making will determine the type of kitchen you need to have.

Three Options for a Licensed Food Production Facility

Thanks to the booming food industry, there are three main options for making food products legally: renting a space, building a commercially approved kitchen in your home or contracting with a co-packer. In all cases, these are licensed, commercial production facilities. Some of these options provide an affordable way to scale up your product in modest ways without having to take on major debt. The following summarizes each.

Option 1: Renting a licensed food production facility

One of the more affordable ways to start selling wholesale quickly is renting an existing licensed facility. This could be an incubator kitchen, an

La Cochina in San Fransisco cultivates food entrepreneurs. JOHN D. IVANKO

existing restaurant or some church kitchens.

(a) A licensed incubator kitchen

Incubator kitchens, sometimes called cooperative or shared-use kitchens, are commercial kitchens that are run in a collaborative fashion. You simply rent the kitchen for an amount of time and use the space and equipment you need.

Incubator kitchens can be operated privately or, more often, by non-profit organizations. Non-profit incubators often provide resources and support in the expansion of your start-up, such as culinary and marketing training and shared office space. Some even have a video production lab that allow business owners to make educational or promotional videos or movies. Many provide networking opportunities among other food entrepreneurs. When you succeed, these incubator kitchens succeed.

For example, Blue Ridge Food Ventures in Asheville, North Carolina, offers 11,000 square feet of shared-use space to support food venture start-ups ranging from value-added products to caterers and food-cart vendors. As a non-profit initiative, Blue Ridge Food Ventures (blueridgefoodventures. org) offers strong support to help fledgling businesses succeed, including everything from storage space and equipment use to label design advice.

The majority of incubator kitchens are located in urban areas, where they can serve a larger population, but rural incubator kitchens are increasing in number as well. Locating a facility may be a challenge, depending on where you live. Check the following website to see if there's one near you: culinaryincubator.com/maps.php.

While incubator kitchens are created to serve small food enterprises, they're not free. Less expensive than building your own commercially licensed kitchen, they rent out their facility by the hour, running from $10 to $40 an hour. A non-profit facility is generally cheaper than a privately owned one.

They may require a minimum block of time and a lease contract; they may also require a detailed business plan, liability insurance and ServSafe certification.

Since rural incubator kitchens rarely experience the same volume of use that urban ones do, they are often run by non-profit organizations that draw on grant support for their operation, one reason they may be a more affordable option. For example, the Starting Block (startingblock.biz), located in rural northwestern Michigan, showcases a partnership of economic

Renting an Incubator, Restaurant or Church Kitchen Checklist

Now that you're scaling up, what should you consider when selecting a commercial kitchen to rent? The following are a few essential questions or issues to consider, arranged as a checklist.

[ ] **Licensing:** Is the kitchen licensed properly for the food product you want to produce there?

[ ] **Equipment:** Does the kitchen have, in proper working order, the equipment you need to make your item in the quantity needed?

[ ] **Storage:** Will you have access to storage space, either refrigerated or on shelves for dry goods? Is storage included in the rental fee, or an additional charge? Is the storage space private and secured, or shared and accessible to others who use the space?

[ ] **Hours of access:** When can you access the kitchen? Are there a minimum number of hours that you must commit to before being able to use the facility?

[ ] **Price:** Are there peak and non-peak rates for the use of the kitchen?

[ ] **Management:** How is the facility managed from the perspective of safety, theft prevention and security? Are others using the facility required to complete ServSafe certification, which might ensure that health and food contamination issues are fully addressed? Generally, how clean and well maintained is the facility? What happens if the equipment you want to use is either inoperable or breaks down while you're using it?

[ ] **Other facility benefits:** What other features are included with the rental of the kitchen? Is telephone, fax, wireless Internet access or business office space included or available for an additional charge?

[ ] **Insurance:** What type and how much insurance must you carry to cover your use of the facility?

[ ] **Miscellaneous fees:** Are there any hidden charges or requirements in the fine print of your contract or lease for renting the facility?

[ ] **Deliveries and lock-outs:** How are food deliveries handled? Should you be receiving ingredients or supplies at the rented facility? What happens if you get locked out of the facility by accident?

development groups and non-profits, who have collaborated to create this resource for food entrepreneurs residing in or near the small town of Hart.

Kitchen rental hours can add up, especially if you're making something like bread with a long rise time. Plus you'll need to account for your time commuting back and forth. If you're raising young children, you'll need to recognize possible daycare needs — and costs.

Storage space at an incubator kitchen may be limited or come at an additional cost. You may find yourself schlepping ingredients and packaging back and forth every time you produce. While the equipment is shared, you'll need to coordinate schedules to avoid any conflicts with others using the space or equipment at the same time as you.

If you specialize in products for customers with food allergies, you'll need to work out the specifics to avoid possible health issues. That said, some incubators, like Prep (prepatl.com) in Atlanta, Georgia, include a commercial kitchen, a USDA-approved meat kitchen and a gluten-free kitchen, each as separate licensed food preparation facilities.

(b) A licensed kitchen from a local church or restaurant

Unless you're operating in a remote, unpopulated area, most food entrepreneurs will be within reach of restaurants or churches that might have licensed kitchen facilities available for rent. Some church kitchens, particularly larger ones that do a lot of public events with meals, go through state commercial inspection. Most of your work can easily be timed not to conflict with church events. To see if one exists near you, check out the website Commercial Kitchen for Rent, commercialkitchen forrent.com.

The same rental arrangement could be made at a local restaurant which, by the fact that it serves food to the public, must undertake extensive health inspections

Sample Kitchen Rental Contract

Whether you're renting an incubator, restaurant or church kitchen, you'll need to negotiate terms and sign a contract that will detail your rental fee. The contract should also detail your responsibility for utility expenses and obligations related to cleanup and proper hygiene. The kitchen will likely require that your business have general and product liability coverage, ranging from $300,000 to $1,000,000, that extends specifically to the kitchen in use; they will request a "certificate of insurance" be issued explicitly naming the rented facility as an additional insured party.

A sample kitchen rental contract can be found on this book's website, homemade forsale.com.

and adhere to all regulations related to the license they hold. Scheduling a mutually agreeable rental period may be your biggest challenge, however, depending on how many hours the restaurant is open every day.

Option 2: Building a commercial kitchen on your home property

If you thrive by operating a home-based business from your kitchen, perhaps while the young kids sleep in the other room, then building a state-approved commercial facility on your home property may be viable, providing you have both the space and funds. This facility could be in your home or possibly another structure located on the property you own.

While comparable, conceptually, to operating a cottage food enterprise in that you're selling products made in your home, the similarities end there. For all practical purposes, going this route means you're turning your home kitchen — or creating a separate facility within your home — into a bona fide commercial kitchen that adheres to the required health code requirements for the food items you're producing.

Without a doubt, this is the most expensive option, and can run from $20,000 to more than $50,000, depending on your plans and goals. What you'll need to renovate will depend on your state and what you plan on making in your kitchen.

The general requirements for building a commercial-grade kitchen include a hand-washing sink separate from the food preparation area along with a three-compartment sink or approved dishwasher for washing equipment and utensils daily. Additionally, floors and walls must be smooth, non-absorbent and easily cleaned; you'll need to check on the specifics within your state. There may be aesthetic considerations, too, since that beautiful granite countertop may need to be replaced with a stainless steel one. Shelving must adhere to strict floor elevation requirements.

When these commercial codes reference "approved" equipment, items that bear the National Sanitation Foundation (NSF) certification, literally "NSF" printed on them, are what you want. This means the manufacturer adhered to strict commercial-food code guidelines. Most mainstream home appliances, such as the home-kitchen refrigerator, bears neither the NSF initials nor adhere to the level of standards required.

Remember, commercial kitchens are not one-size-fits-all. Commercial kitchens in your state do not all have the same equipment or specifics;

Jamming Expansion: Building an On-farm Commercial Kitchen

Name: Dorothy Stainbrook

Business: HeathGlen's Farm & Kitchen (Forest Lake, Minnesota)

Website: heathglen.com

Products: preserves, syrups, shrubs

Sales Venue: farmers' market

Annual Sales: $25,000+

"Your best research comes directly from your customers. Ask them what they like and make it," shares Dorothy Stainbrook, owner of HeathGlen's Farm & Kitchen, specializing in preserves, syrups and shrubs made from the organic fruit from her farm.

Stainbrook lives the lesson behind this advice: she first launched and tested her jams at farmers' markets in Minneapolis and St. Paul while operating under Minnesota's cottage food law. Thanks to customer feedback, Stainbrook found a niche in unique preserve flavor combos like blueberry lavender with merlot wine. With this sales success moving her closer to her state's gross sales cap, she expanded and invested in building an on-farm commercial kitchen.

To understand and learn from Stainbrook's evolution, jump back to 1998. "Our five-year-old daughter at the time had some medical problems that needed Mom to stay closer to home. As I gazed out the window at our 23 acres, even though those fallow fields were at the time overgrown with weeds, I saw an opportunity to trade my white-collar career and follow my true dream of starting a farm." HeathGlen Organic Farm erupted from this vision, five acres of primarily berries along with herbs and vegetables sold at the St. Paul and Mill City Farmers' Markets from May through December.

"Almost ten years later, in 2005, that same daughter that turned me into a farmer decided some jellies would be nice for the peanut butter sandwiches she took to swim practice," recalls Stainbrook. "Turns out we had a bumper crop of fruit that year, so I confess I went a little overboard trying all kinds of pepper, wine and fruit jellies."

This value-added direction proved to be something Stainbrook could readily experiment with under Minnesota's cottage food law and strongly fit with her future business vision: "I wanted HeathGlen to be more than a hobby; I wanted to make a full living on the farm," explains Stainbrook. "I saw these fruit preserves as an opportunity to develop a part of the farm business that would take me through the whole year financially, especially the winter months."

HeathGlen owner Dorothy Stainbrook in her commercially licensed home kitchen.
COURTESY OF HEATHGLEN'S FARM & KITCHEN

"I did a ton of sampling at the market to get feedback from customers while developing a unique distinction by keeping the sugar as low as I could. This really accents the fresh fruit flavor." Stainbrook also tapped into her former bartending expertise and blended liquors into the preserves to enhance the fruit flavor. Volume and sales snowballed to the point that Stainbrook exceeded the $5,000 Minnesota gross sales cap in 2008 and needed to look into commercial kitchen venues.

"I first rented commercial kitchen space at a local church that had a state license and had rented to businesses like mine before," explains Stainbrook. "Even though this kitchen space was just a mile away, I quickly realized the hassle in packing and lugging my ingredients and equipment back and forth from the rented space. I also hated being away from my kids who were young at the time, and I also needed to be on-farm to supervise my staff of part-time employees."

After two years of the church kitchen arrangement, Stainbrook decided to build a commercial facility on her farm. "If you grow your own produce and don't have on-site storage at your rented kitchen venue — always my situation — building your own commercial kitchen may make sense from an efficiency standpoint."

Stainbrook is quick to advise the importance of patience and understanding the time and cost involved with building such a facility. "I was the first on-farm facility that many of my state regulators had to work with, so we were often learning together on what, exactly, this needed to look like. I love what I have now, but there were lots of hurdles and expense to get here." It took her about two years total to build her kitchen, including one year in the planning and permit state and a second year to actually build it.

Signage at HeathGlen's Farm & Kitchen farmstand, including suggested cheese and jam pairing ideas.
COURTESY OF HEATHGLEN'S FARM & KITCHEN

HeathGlen's Farm & Kitchen syrups displayed at a farmers' market stand.
COURTESY OF HEATHGLEN'S FARM & KITCHEN

The kitchen is built within the existing attached garage, but needed things like a new floor, walls and lights to reach code for the state of Minnesota.

A reality of plowing new ground with state regulations is that Heath-Glen Farm needed to comply with a litany of requirements, even if these stipulations were overkill for this small canned food business. "To comply with different regulations, we definitely built more than we realistically needed. We had an additional handicap-accessible bathroom, even through I was the only one working here. A huge ventilation intake system covers a six-foot area over the stove, which is overkill for the size of the kitchen space." The commercial kitchen cost about $50,000, which was financed by family savings. The highest kitchen expense was a large ventilation system which she rarely uses.

The new kitchen was a playground for product experimentation. With the growing market interest among foodies in "craft cocktails," Stainbrook tapped into her bartending background and started making fruit-flavored syrups and shrubs, a vinegar-based fruit sugar syrup that dates back to colonial times. She sells these jarred value-added products at both summer and winter farmers' markets. The winter sales average higher, at around two hundred jars per event. The jars sell for eight dollars for a half-pint jar of preserves, and the syrups are also eight dollars, for an eight-ounce bottle.

With the new syrup and shrub additions, Stainbrook realized the importance of customer education to showcase and highlight how her products could be used. A "Balcony Bartender Blog" features short You - Tube videos demonstrating how to use the products in craft cocktails. She also actively maintains a recipe blog that offers creative ways to incorporate her products into various dishes, all of which can be accessed off her website.

"With the success of my preserve business, it led to the expansion and the advent of the new product lines of syrups and shrubs because I could process these at home," Stainbrook adds. "I'm thankful for cottage food laws. As a farmer, I didn't have the money or the time resources to go into the city and rent a commercial kitchen when I got started."

HeathGlen owner Dorothy Stainbrook in front of her farmers' market stand. Courtesy of HeathGlen's Farm & Kitchen

it depends on what food item you'll be producing and in what quantity. Generally, the simpler and less processed your item, the less costly and complicated a commercial kitchen setup will be.

Want to simply grow your existing cottage food business? Because these operations focus on low-risk, non-hazardous food, creating a commercial kitchen to make your jam or bake your cookies will not be complicated. While not a cheap endeavor, a kitchen for these products will not require the same level of equipment or infrastructure as one for producing fried meat pies or prepared meals. Many states provide a specific commercial kitchen classification, called "bakery," that outlines this simpler kitchen licensing and required setup.

When dealing with your state agency, if the inspector tells you that you need a costly piece of equipment that doesn't apply to what you are producing — say, an excessive stovetop venting system when all you are doing is making jam — speak up. Nicely, of course. Ask for an "exemption" to a specific requirement and give specific estimated usage data to validate your case. Or buy yourself some time and enquire if this issue could be revisited in a year to determine if it's really necessary based on your actual operational history.

Option 3: Working with a contract packer, or co-packer

A contract packer, or co-packer, is a company that processes food products, either using their surplus capacity or specializing in packing other businesses' food items. You turn over your recipe, perhaps some ingredients if you're growing them yourself, and any other marketing elements and the co-packer takes it from there. What you get in return is a ready-to-sell product.

Depending on the co-packers, they might provide the following services:

- Production of the product
- Guidance on product formulation and development, including reformulating home recipes to large-scale production processes
- Packaging of the product
- Guidance on aspects of labeling, especially related to regulatory requirements
- Advice related to marketing and distribution

From a time and labor perspective, if you have customers lining up to place orders or a confirmed wholesale outlet, this route allows you to scale up without investing in or renting a commercial kitchen. You take your recipe and ingredient list to a co-packer that specializes in the food product you make and they produce it for you. Due to the volume produced, this may afford greater consistency of your product, quality and economies of scale realized through purchasing power, among other benefits. Additionally, co-packers can assist with the requirements that arise as you move from being a small cottage food enterprise to a wholesaler, including UPC codes, nutritional labeling and any lab analysis that may be required, covered briefly in the next chapter.

Going with a co-packer comes with a higher per unit cost. You will need to evaluate this increase in terms of time, labor and the financial resources required to produce your items another way. If this streamlined and complete process of production seems too good to be true, don't forget the price and minimum order requirement.

Sandhill Family Farms' Organic Pureed Tomato made with the farm's organic tomatoes but processed by a local co-packer. Courtesy of Sandhill Family Farms

For example, Sandhill Family Farms in Brodhead, Wisconsin, uses a local co-packer that specializes in items that are "pumped," such as sauces, to turn their extra tomatoes into canned organic pureed tomatoes. While the final product they received is labeled and ready for wholesale, Matt and Peg Sheaffer, who run the farm, choose to use most of the jars to add a little surprise extra to member share boxes of their CSA (community supported agriculture) in the early spring, when the boxes can sometimes run a little lean as the harvest hasn't fully kicked in yet. The key with co-packers is that they typically require a large minimum produce volume with which to work. For the Sheaffers, their co-packer requires a minimum of five thousand pounds of tomatoes.

Loss of control over much of the process deters some food entrepreneurs from going in this direction. While appealing in its efficiency, the quality and flavor may not perfectly match what you feel you could do yourself. Your recipe will no longer be handmade, in your kitchen. Co-packers have very efficient means to produce items at significant economies of scale through factory-oriented processes. Therefore, you'll need to verify that your label goes on your product made with your recipe — and not just slapped on jars of "strawberry-rhubarb jam" made by the co-packer.

In the final chapter, we'll explore in more detail some of the marketing possibilities, changes in your operations and sources of funding to make your culinary hit a reality.

*Sharing samples at a retail store selling
both baked goods and canned products.*
JOHN D. IVANKO

14

Multiple Markets and Money Matters

A S YOU RAMP UP YOUR PRODUCTION along the continuum of scaling up your operations — perhaps moving from your home kitchen to a rented kitchen or renovated commercial space on your property — you'll need to be particularly attentive to every aspect of your business. The scope of your operations, importance of marketing — especially packaging and pricing — and impact of competition will all be magnified.

At this point, profit is no longer a given, and the potential for financial failure can be devastating if you don't have a carefully devised and thorough plan in place. Once you head down the path of renting or building your own commercial kitchen or contracting out to a co-packer to produce your product for you, you may find that being the baker, canner or granola bar-maker takes a back seat to running the business itself. This may be a great thing or take you away from what you love most: having your fingers in real dough.

There's also the opportunity to hit the specialty food Powerball with your product or create a viable and exciting full-time enterprise that makes a career in a cubicle obsolete. There's the possibility to pull in a six-figure salary or sell off your enterprise and retire a millionaire. You may be putting your cookies up against Famous Amos or Mrs. Fields. Markets are everywhere, and funds to fuel your expansion may be just a click away, thanks to new "crowdsourcing" financing options available on the Internet.

This chapter will delve into a few of the many market opportunities open to you. It explores some realities regarding how your operations must change by default of your expansion plans and the regulatory environment you now face. It also provides some financial avenues you might want to pursue, outside a commercial loan from a bank. At this stage of the game, there's no such thing as a one-size-fits-all strategy.

As mentioned previously, we've written this book for entry-level food entrepreneurs. We'll leave it to other books and resources already available for a more exhaustive examination of issues related to your expansion into a full-blown, full-time food enterprise.

Markets, Markets Everywhere

In a licensed food production facility and with a food processor permit, you can sell wholesale, potentially to the world. As discussed earlier in this book, some cottage food laws also permit sales via indirect or wholesale channels. Your markets could be specialty stores; institutions like schools, restaurants, hospitals or supermarkets, or by mail order only. Your choice may be limited only by your financial means, access to capital, energy level or perseverance.

In many cases, when CFOs grow big, they're selling products wholesale in the specialty food industry, defined by the Specialty Food Association as:

> foods and beverages that exemplify quality, innovation and style in their category. Their specialty nature derives from some or all of the following characteristics: their originality, authenticity, ethnic or cultural origin, specific processing, ingredients, limited supply, distinctive use, extraordinary packaging or specific channel of distribution or sale. By virtue of their differentiation in their categories, such products maintain a high perceived value and often command a premium price.

Specialty foods are hot, according to the Specialty Food Association; sales have grown 22 percent between 2010 and 2012 and topped $85 billion in 2012. Grocery retailers are the primary distribution of specialty food products, but such products can also be sold through other channels including some already familiar to CFOs, namely farmers' markets and by direct order.

Grocery Retailers

Your packaged products may line the shelves of grocery stores, gourmet food shops and specialty food retailers, large and small. Regional specialty food stores, food cooperatives and other retailers might focus on health foods, specialty foods, seasonal or year-round gifts or items that are made locally or regionally.

Included among the list of retailers might be the following:

- Supermarkets, like Safeway, Kroger and BI-LO
- Specialty natural foods grocers, like Whole Foods Market and The Fresh Market
- Big-box retailers, like Costco and Sam's Club

To reach these retailers, one of the more effective routes to market your products will likely be through exhibiting at a trade show where you can take orders from retailers or distributors in the markets you wish to serve.

Direct-to-customer Sales

When you scale up to a point where boxes of product become cases or pallets, you'll need a sales force to accomplish what you once did yourself. No one can be in two or more places at the same time, so plan on hiring sales staff to work your booths or fulfill orders as they come in via telephone, text or the Internet. When selling wholesale, many food entrepreneurs contract with brokers who take a commission on every order they secure on your behalf.

Mail Order

By producing in a licensed commercial kitchen facility, suddenly you can ship your product to customers anywhere they can receive a package within the US. Packaging your product for safe transport, plus the added cost and labor associated with such, will be important variables to consider when determining a viable and profitable business model.

Mail-order specialty food catalogs are another route to reach out to potential first-time customers. Getting one or more of your products listed in these catalogs may be a relatively affordable way to build relationships with new customers.

Institutions Serving Patrons

Institutional sales may include supplying schools, restaurants, hotels and, even, hospitals. Sales to these outlets are for consumption by the patrons

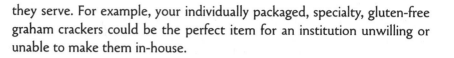

they serve. For example, your individually packaged, specialty, gluten-free graham crackers could be the perfect item for an institution unwilling or unable to make them in-house.

From Handmade to Mechanized

If you found it challenging to put your peal-and-stick labels on fifty packages of biscuits, tidy and straight, try it with a thousand — or ten thousand. Cutting attractive cloth tops and adding a nice ribbon for a box of twelve jelly jars becomes overwhelming when an order comes in for a case of 240 jars. When you scale up, you'll be forced to re-evaluate the systems and procedures you put into place for your once-small cottage food enterprise.

Depending on the degree at which you expand, you might find that new equipment in the kitchen or office becomes a necessary part of delivering a consistent, professional-looking product. The three hundred to seven hundred dollars you'll end up paying for various label machines, depending on your type of packaging, will improve the presentation of your product and save on labor costs. For example, a label machine designed for various styles of containers from Zap Labeler (zaplabeler.com) can pay for itself on labor costs within the year, plus improve the consistency of the application of the label; having crooked or misplaced labels must be avoided when serving any retail markets. Some machines can take self-adhesive roll labels and attach them to as many as one thousand containers in one hour.

Labeling for the Big Leagues

Attaching a cute, homemade label printed off from your color laser-jet printer to your packet of dried seasonings mix may have worked just fine for most cottage food laws. But when you're selling wholesale, meticulously following the US Food and Drug Administration (FDA) label requirements is a must; download it from the FDA at fda.gov. The nutritional label must conform to Title 21 of the Code of Federal Regulations and include a nutritional fact analysis. Only food companies with "annual gross sales made or business done in sales to consumers that is not more than $500,000 or have annual gross sales made or business done in sales of food to consumers of not more than $50,000 are exempt," according to the FDA. As discussed earlier and related to specialty food production, the only other exemption,

"One of the greatest strengths small food businesses have is the ability to think and quickly act outside of standard business models to meet customer needs in new and unique ways. This might include providing healthy snacks to corporations for their employees, creating subscriber-based food boxes based on a CSA-business model either alone or with other artisan food entrepreneurs ... adding new flavor profiles to your product line, or hundreds of other ideas. Don't be afraid to mix business models like you mix ingredients, searching for the right combination that will catch consumers' interest."

— 2014 PLATE OF THE UNION REPORT, SMALL FOOD BUSINESS (SMALLFOODBIZ.COM)

per the US FDA, is for products sold at a low volume. The exemption applies:

> *"if the person claiming the exemption employs fewer than an average of 100 full-time equivalent employees and fewer than 100,000 units of that product are sold in the United States in a 12-month period. To qualify for this exemption the person must file a notice annually with FDA…. If a person is not an importer, and has fewer than 10 full-time equivalent employees, that person does not have to file a notice for any food product with annual sales of fewer than 10,000 total units…. If any nutrient content claim (e.g., "sugar free"), health claim, or other nutrition information is provided on the label, or in labeling or advertising, the small business exemption is not applicable for a product."*

Securing the required FDA nutritional labels need not cost a fortune, however. ReciPal (recipal.com) provides an affordable, online nutritional label creator software option, providing FDA-compliant nutritional fact labels and ingredient lists. The company also offers recipe costing by batch and package. Best of all, it was designed by food entrepreneurs for food entrepreneurs.

Those CFOs able and eager to sell via wholesale accounts will need a UPC Code, covered in Chapter 5. You may also need to secure a SKU or stock keeping unit, an eight-digit alpha-numeric code unique to your product that's different than an UPC Code, a string of twelve numbers that's standardized for business use and able to be scanned. A company could have different SKUs but the same UPC code for a particular product. Did we mention things get more complex at this stage?

In some cases, if you opt to use a co-packer, the work you did packaging, labeling and ingredient sourcing may require revisions; you may need to completely redo your product based on licensing regulations or standards dictated to you by the industry, distribution channels or markets you serve.

Pricing and Distribution Revisited: A Whole New Formula

Like many other facets of your business, when you scale up and sell wholesale, you change the dynamic of your profit margins since other businesses

need to make money off selling your product. You may need to revise your pricing structures to incentivize initial orders.

While your product might retail for eight dollars (also referred to as the "suggested retail price"), you'll only receive a portion of that to allow the retailer and distributor to each make some money along the way. At this point, your profits are based largely on the volume of product you can move through your distribution and retail channels. You're forfeiting some profit per item when you sell through indirect channels.

When it comes to distribution, most CFOs evaluate their market in terms of a region, if not a city or neighborhood. When scaling up, they'll determine if they'll select a third-party distributor; ship via FedEx, UPS or the US postal service; or deliver their products themselves. Third-party distributors often require a 15 to 30 percent markup over wholesale cost and may do their own ordering and invoicing with retailers they supply with your products.

In some cases, you may find retailers will only work through distributors. That means, to get your product to market, you have to entice distributors to stock and sell your items. As a result, many companies with specialty food products head to trade shows to prospect for companies willing to carry their items.

Keep in mind, just because you can sell your gingersnaps nationally to five hundred specialty food stores doesn't mean you actually will or that the process will be a fun ride. Beyond the scope of this book, you'll need to sort out shelf-life issues, buy-by dates and have a product recall plan in place.

Magnifying Your Marketing

Much of what we've covered in this book related to marketing serves you well as you scale up your enterprise. However, if your sales forecast is $100,000, or 40,000 units, it's a good bet that you'll need to radically step up your marketing budget. At this phase, word of mouth remains essential, but boosting awareness with a PR campaign, setting up food sampling demos at specialty food retailers or exploring more traditional advertising outlets may be necessary to introduce potential customers to your products. This can cost big bucks. Depending on your product, prospecting for national distributors mean you'll be packing your bags and heading to a specialty food trade show.

Margins, Markup, Warehousing and Freight Costs

For food entrepreneurs selling wholesale, the distribution channels open up in ways that allow hundreds of thousands of potential customers to buy your products. Getting your items to market, however, may require the services of distributors, co-packers, food brokers or a sales force. There are variations in commissions and fees based on your product, season, market and a host of other variables.

The goal for your business should always be to earn some profit after you deduct your expenses, both variable and fixed. In terms of the cost of your product, you'll also need to account for any freight expenses and commissions charged along the distribution channel, plus allow yourself a "fair" profit on each product sold at the end of the day. Of course, there are other expenses you'll need to account for as well, including "shrinkage" from shoplifting or errors in shipping, any sales discounts you may offer and changes in ingredient costs. Your "cost of goods sold," or COGS, refers to the variable and fixed costs that go into making your product. The details are beyond the scope of this book, but suffice it to say that if you're taking orders for ten thousand units, you'll need to have a very good handle on your COGS for each item you sell and your margins. Whatever price you list as the suggested retail price, you'll need to allow for 50 to 65 percent margin above your wholesale price so the different brokers, distributors and retailers can each have their cut when they sell your product.

Since some companies may be storing your products in warehouses, there are costs associated with this service. To get your product to a distributor's warehouse, the freight cost may be included in the price, collected separately at the time of delivery or added to your original invoice. The "ex-warehouse cost" combines the cost of your product with the storage and handling costs.

While the market and your customers ultimately determine the retail price you're able to charge for your product, when coming up with a price, you'll need to analyze both your profit margin and markup to account for whatever distribution channel or channels you decide to pursue, each summarized below.

- **Gross margin, or margin:** An expression for a percentage of a selling price. It's the difference between total sales of an item and the cost associated with those sales.

  Example: One jar of jam sells for $6, but costs $2 to make; the gross margin is $4. Expressed as a percentage, the margin would be 67 percent. The math: $((6 - 2) / 6) \times 100 = 67$ percent.

- **Markup:** An expression for a percentage of the cost for a product. It's the selling price of the item minus the cost, then divided by the cost associated with those sales.

  Example: Using the same numbers, one jar of jam sells for $6, but costs $2 to make; the markup is $4. Expressed as a percentage, the markup would be 200 percent. The math: $((6 - 2) / 2) \times 100 = 200$ percent.

Again, beyond the scope of this book, careful analysis of this entire distribution chain and pricing in relation to your competition is essential to increasing your likelihood of financial success — profitability!

Profile

The Happy Tomato: Bringing Back Spaghetti Night

Name: Liz James

Business: The Happy Tomato (Charlottesville, Virginia)

Website: thehappytomatoes.com

Products: tomato marinara and pizza sauce

Sales Venue: wholesale to local retailers

Sales: $50,000+

Liz with a jar of The Happy Tomato's Marinara sauce.

<small>Courtesy of the Happy Tomato</small>

It's no lofty claim found on the Happy Tomato label — "It's the sauce that makes a difference." Owner Liz James set out to launch a home-based food business that can turn lives around. Even her own.

James' vision for the Happy Tomato goes beyond a simple profit motive. She sees her sauce playing a role in getting families back together again and connecting around the supper table through a simple, quick, healthy meal. "Heat up my sauce, boil some noodles, add some bread and a salad and — poof — you have an economical meal that brings people together," she explains.

James lucked out by living in Virginia, a state that has cottage food laws for small-scale start-ups and also offers a home food processor license that basically allows her to operate like a commercial operation, but in her home kitchen.

James went through the home food processor route from the get-go for her sauce. While this involved more steps, inspections and fees, James could quickly and efficiently move to her goal of selling wholesale. With a home processor license, a food entrepreneur in Virginia has no gross sales cap and can produce a wide range of items, including foods that would be considered hazardous under cottage food law such as refrigerated items.

"Getting my jarred sauce officially approved for retail sale was a long and complicated process," admits James. The steps included taking an intense online course with the FDA that lasted several days, developing a Universal Product Code (UPC) and having the product tested for food safety. "I'm fortunate that my state of Virginia really works with small entrepreneurs to grow our businesses, providing resources and people to answer questions as I navigated the start-up phase."

Her story exemplifies how deep a role local resources and support can play in championing start-up success. "Hands down, I wouldn't be here today without the support of my local community in Charlottesville, Virginia," proclaims James. Various non-profit groups such as the Community Investment Collaborative (CIC) provided business plan workshops and marketing advice. She also finds the local food entrepreneur community very collaborative, sharing advice and marketing insight.

"Focus on the quality and not the quantity of different types of products," advises James. She does this by purchasing local and seasonal produce direct from as many area farmers as possible. She concentrates on creating just two consistent, premium-priced products: marina sauce and pizza sauce, a smoother version of her marinara sauce. "These two basic sauces can be used over pasta or pizza, or could be dressed up in various ways, from adding meat for a lasagna filling to a sauce for fish." The quart jars retail for $9.99 to $10.99, and James takes back any empty glass canning jars to clean, sterilize and reuse, eager to save money and avoid waste anywhere she can. The stores collect the jars and give the customers one dollar for the return. James then reimburses the stores this dollar.

Funding support came by way of a $2,500 Kiva Zip loan to purchase jars, supplies and a stockpot range. Kiva Zip is a project within Kiva in which the general public serves as "lenders" and collectively makes microfinance loans directly to borrowers like the Happy Tomato via the Internet. Kiva uses these person-to-person funding techniques to garner small contributions as low as five dollars from the general public.

The Happy Tomato's canned marinara sauce that helps create "moments and memories one jar at a time." Jars are sold at Whole Foods Market and other retailers. Courtesy of the Happy Tomato

For James, the big advantage was the loan being interest-free, to be repaid in 24 months. James went through an application process, using the CIC as her official trustee to endorse her loan application. This loan was then also matched by Capital One for the total of $5,000. Much more personal than a bank loan, Kiva Zip offers a "conversations" feature on the borrower's Kiva site that enables entrepreneurs like James to connect with and receive cheerleading from the folks that supported her loan, people who also do not receive interest but help champion and feel a part of start-ups like the Happy Tomato.

When James launched in 2012 and sold Happy Tomato sauces direct to customers at local farmers' markets, she quickly learned the importance of sampling. "If people could taste my product, they'd immediately experience the special flavors and were willing to pay a premium price." Her sauce is based off an old Sicilian family recipe, using plum tomatoes, extra virgin olive oil, onion, garlic, basil, rosemary and other spices.

While she sold direct to customers at the farmers' market, James simultaneously built a wholesale business selling to area retailers, including Whole Foods Market. By 2014 she had transitioned exclusively to wholesale and was focusing her marketing efforts on in-store demonstrations and sampling. "I found my biggest bang for my time was when I do in-store sampling. Shoppers are much more likely to walk away with jars of my product," adds James.

"Whole Foods Market has been a great company to work with. My experience is they truly step out of the regular corporate fray and exemplify a sincere commitment to local sourcing," James shares. She's excited about a Whole Foods Market-driven initiative locally to help establish a community warehouse for various regional food products like hers. "This will help tremendously as various retail accounts can access my product whenever they need to restock, and I will save time by not always driving around and delivering." Her contacts at Whole Foods also proved to be extremely helpful in providing business and product feedback and advice as well as referrals to other retailer accounts.

"I'm big on slow yet steady growth," admits James. "After my first year, I asked myself, 'Do I have a lemonade hobby stand or a company that is viable to generate my full-time income?' I'm committed to make this business work and know I need to build enough regular wholesale accounts to grow into a commercial kitchen situation."

Thanks to loyal retail accounts like Whole Foods Market, the Happy Tomato is growing closer to James' goal of producing 135 to 150 cases (12 units per case) weekly, which she calculated would enable her to scale up to a commercial facility and hire more help. James held several part-time jobs as she launched and grew the Happy Tomato and is slowly peeling back and eliminating these as her sauce profit grows.

"For the first time in my life, I'm earning income while simultaneously doing something I truly believe in: providing a reason and a means for getting the family around the dinner table again," sums up James. "You can't beat that feeling of satisfaction at the end of the day."

A plate of pasta with sauce from The Happy Tomato.
COURTESY OF THE HAPPY TOMATO

Raising Some Dough

Any way you slice it, expanding your business will take more money than you needed to launch your business out of your home kitchen. There are numerous opportunities, however, to expand your production and marketing without going into major debt. If you decided to expand your operations modestly, the profits from your cottage food enterprise may have stayed in your business checking account as retained earnings, providing some or all of the funds needed for re-investing in your growth. Depending on your goals and ambitions, you may, or may not, need to refinance your home to secure funds to take your business up the next notch along that continuum of scaling up.

If your business or personal sources for money aren't enough, you may consider a growing number of financial resources that have nothing to do with a commercial bank. Called "crowdfunding," these mostly Internet-based sources of financing can provide small low-interest loans or thousands of dollars, depending on your needs and if you have the knack to create compelling, engaging fundraising campaigns and a customer base eager to support your dream with their open pocketbooks. The following summarizes a few of your options for financing.

- **Kiva: kiva.org**

  More personal and accessible than a bank loan, Kiva taps the wealth of private individuals who fund small business with low-interest loans. You apply for a loan and share your story with prospective lenders who, through an online portal, decide if your venture is worth funding. The Kiva Zip Loan program is for smaller $5,000 to $20,000 interest-free loans; these loans need to be paid back to the bank within six to sixty months, depending on the loan size. Kiva also offers larger loans that carry interest.

- **Kickstarter: kickstarter.com**

  The world's largest Internet-based, privately owned crowdfunding platform, Kickstarter supports a wide range of creative projects, including food products. Backers pledge various amounts of money in exchange for various incentives, called "backer rewards," associated with different levels of funding support. One bakery start-up launched a $10,000

campaign which, if funded, would pay for ingredients and manufacturing costs for their first major production run of three product items, initial packaging costs, FDA-approved database nutrition fact analysis and SKUs for each flavor.

- **Indiegogo: indiegogo.com**
  Another Internet-based crowdfunding website that includes a food category. "Backers" receive "perks" with their financial contribution.

- **Slow Money Alliance: slowmoney.org**
  A grassroots-led, invest-local, non-profit organization that has poured millions of small private donor funds into food-related small enterprises in communities where various Slow Money chapters exist. Most of the funding supports small farm needs or local food distribution systems. Promising food enterprises register for an Entrepreneur Showcase, where they have the opportunity to formally pitch their business idea and funding need to potential investors.

- **Kabbage: kabbage.com**
  From $500 to $100,000, Kabbage provides working capital online to currently operating businesses, based on the extension of a business line of credit. Interest rates vary from 1 percent to 13.5 percent.

- **Small Business Administration's microloan program: sba.gov**
  Government-backed loans to small businesses up to $50,000, made available through certain non-profit, community-based organizations. Rates for the six-year term loans range from 8 to 13 percent.

Keep Tabs

When scaling up, the volume and complexity of the business will expand exponentially — especially if you're juggling employees, various sub-contractors, relationships with multiple distributors and retailers and the stepped-up governmental requirements that come with a business your size.

For bookkeeping, a software program like Intuit's Quickbooks will become indispensable. If you're a baker consider CakeBoss (cakeboss.com), a software program customized for a specialty baked goods business. If you're big on wholesale with distributors and direct retailer relationships, you might consider Komida (komida.com), an online order management system for specialty food manufacturers.

At this point, hiring a certified public accountant is a must. Retaining an attorney for legal matters is a wise decision, too. With your graduation from cottage food enterprise to food corporation, you've earned the right to hire professionals to steer you clear of possible financial or legal problems.

Additionally, that network of mentors who helped your business get off the ground will likely be reinforced by a board of directors and other managerial staff who you've invited aboard to help guide the growth of your business. Many hands helping to keep tabs will afford you the time you need to see your dream to fruition.

Attractive packaging showcases Kika's Treats, 100% handmade.
JOHN D. IVANKO

Epilogue
Icing on the Cake

*H*OMEMADE FOR SALE offers a snapshot of the growing cottage food business movement and the opportunities and the possibilities it offers. Thousands of home cooks are embracing the idea of launching their own food enterprise. Many already have, captured by the inspiring "story profiles" found woven into the how-to text; these cookiepreneurs and profitable picklers have made their dreams come true. Throughout these pages, we have also shared snippets of our own experiences at our home and business, Inn Serendipity Bed & Breakfast and farm in southwestern Wisconsin.

Our motivation to create a start-up resource guide for cottage food operators stems from our interest to nurture a nation of enterprising citizens. But our personal connection to the movement runs deeper than earning a little extra income by selling pickles, and hopefully baked goods, from our home kitchen.

We see food as a path to freedom and happiness in multiple ways. Back in our twenties, we did everything "right" according to our family, the media and society. We commuted to corporate cubicles, received a bi-monthly paycheck and bought shrink-wrapped groceries and take-out meals packed in Styrofoam containers. We lived tethered to the system, dependent on others for everything from our paycheck to our dinner menu.

We discovered early on, however, that this path wasn't for us. When we took the big leap in 1996 and moved to our five acres in Wisconsin, we planted our first zucchini seed in the garden that following spring. Playing a joke that only Mother Nature can play, those initial zucchini seeds never sprouted. But we kept planting. And planting. The following seasons brought both bountiful garden harvests and increasing morning muffin baking as we learned, challenged ourselves and grew in multiple ways. We realized and embraced the independence that comes with connecting with both our food source and our entrepreneurial spirit. These two forces

Inn Serendipity house. JOHN D. IVANKO

empowered us and peppered our lives with creativity, passion and the satisfaction that comes with growing, preparing and savoring our own meals, usually around the dining room table with our son, family or friends.

That intoxicating combination of food and self-employment transformed our lives and drives us to share this elixir with others, with you, through *Homemade for Sale*. The truth emerged from our jar of pickles and bread, still warm from the oven: we found our happiness in the foods we shared and the life we created around our passions for nourishing ourselves and sustaining the planet.

For more on our story, please see our other books: *Rural Renaissance, ECOpreneuring* and *Farmstead Chef.* In the pages of *Homemade for Sale,* we aspired to provoke, inspire and inform. We essayed to provide both a launching pad for your dream business built around your passions and offer a toolkit for you to start your own cottage food venture. The passage of the cottage food laws enables just about anyone, anywhere, to turn their home-cooked passion into some profits and revitalize their local economy.

We invite you to share your story, idea or inspiration on the website created for this book: homemadeforsale.com. And look for us in line at your holiday bazaar or farmers' market stand — or clicking "Like" on your Facebook page.

Together, we can change the way America eats.

Index

About the Authors

Lisa Kivirist

AS A PIONEER IN THE COTTAGE FOOD INDUSTRY, both covering the national movement for publications as well as championing for the passage of a "Cookie Bill" in Wisconsin, **Lisa Kivirist** is on the cusp of the latest trends. Lisa and her husband and co-author-and-photographer, **John D. Ivanko**, are food-loving entrepreneurs.

As authors of thirteen books, national speakers and recognized spokespeople for the national sustainable agriculture movement, Lisa and John are regular presenters at numerous national conferences and library, university and community events. They're co-authors of *Farmstead Chef,* the award-winning *ECOpreneuring* and *Rural Renaissance.* John is also the co-author of several award-winning children's multicultural photobooks, including *To Be a Kid, Be My Neighbor* and *To Be an Artist.*

Lisa and John are both sought-after experts for the media. They've been featured in the *New York Times, USA Today, Conde Nast Traveler,* MSNBC and on various radio programs across the country, including Martha Stewart Radio, the Sirius Satellite network and "Good Food" on KCRW. As freelance journalists, they're contributors to *Mother Earth News, Urban Farm, Mother Earth Living, Hobby Farms* and *Natural Awakenings,* among many others. Lisa is a columnist for Hobby Farms and both have a "farmstead chef" blog for Hobbyfarms.com. They also blog for MotherEarthNews. com.

Food Advocacy and Entrepreneurship

Lisa is a distinguished Kellogg Food and Society Policy Fellow and a national advocate and leader for women in sustainable agriculture. She initiated and directs the Rural Women's Project of the Midwest Organic and Sustainable Education Service (mosesorganic.org/projects/rural-womens-project/), an award-winning initiative providing resources and networking for women farmers and food-based entrepreneurs. She writes a column for the Women,

Food and Agriculture Network (WFAN) entitled "Female Fare," connecting women in agriculture to national policy issues.

Pioneers of Farm-Fresh Culinary and Green Travel

Lisa and John are innkeepers of the award-winning Inn Serendipity Bed & Breakfast, completely powered by renewable energy. Their B&B features local, seasonal vegetarian cuisine prepared with ingredients harvested from the Inn's organic gardens. For more, see innserendipity.com. They also write and speak about culinary travel and ecotourism trends.

Lisa and John share their organic farm in Browntown, Wisconsin, with their son, a ten-kilowatt Bergey wind turbine and millions of ladybugs.

You can connect with Lisa and John on Facebook and LinkedIn.

Lisa Kivirist with carrot on farm completely powered by wind and sun.
JOHN D. IVANKO

If you have enjoyed *Homemade for Sale,* you might also enjoy other

BOOKS TO BUILD A NEW SOCIETY

Our books provide positive solutions for people who want to
make a difference. We specialize in:

**Sustainable Living • Green Building • Peak Oil • Renewable Energy
Environment & Economy • Natural Building & Appropriate Technology
Progressive Leadership • Resistance and Community
Educational & Parenting Resources**

New Society Publishers

ENVIRONMENTAL BENEFITS STATEMENT

New Society Publishers has chosen to produce this book on recycled paper made with
100% post consumer waste, processed chlorine free, and old growth free.

For every 5,000 books printed, New Society saves the following resources:[1]

33	Trees
3,018	Pounds of Solid Waste
3,321	Gallons of Water
4,331	Kilowatt Hours of Electricity
5,486	Pounds of Greenhouse Gases
24	Pounds of HAPs, VOCs, and AOX Combined
8	Cubic Yards of Landfill Space

[1]Environmental benefits are calculated based on research done by the Environmental Defense Fund and
other members of the Paper Task Force who study the environmental impacts of the paper industry.

For a full list of NSP's titles, please call 1-800-567-6772 *or check out our website* at:

www.newsociety.com